A MASTERCLASS in
NEEDLE FELTING ENDANGERED SPECIES

METHODS AND TECHNIQUES TO TAKE YOUR NEEDLE FELTING TO THE NEXT LEVEL

Cindy-Lou Thompson

Hubble & Hattie

The Hubble & Hattie imprint offers a range of books that cover all things animal, promoting compassion, understanding and respect between all animals (including humans!)

Also in this series
A Masterclass in Needle Felting Dogs (Thompson)
A Masterclass in Needle Felting Wildlife (Thompson)

Some more great books from Hubble & Hattie!
Animal Grief: How animals mourn (Alderton)
Cat and Dog Health, The Complete Book of (Hansen)
Complete Dog Massage Manual, The – Gentle Dog Care (Robertson)
Confessions of a veterinary nurse: paws, claws and puppy dog tails (Ison)
Detector Dog – A Talking Dogs Scentwork Manual (Mackinnon)
Dinner with Rover: delicious, nutritious meals for you and your dog to share (Paton-Ayre)
Dog Cookies: healthy, allergen-free treat recipes for your dog (Schöps)
Emergency First Aid for dogs: at home and away Revised Edition (Bucksch)
Fun and Games for Cats (Seidl)
Gods, ghosts, and black dogs – the fascinating folklore and mythology of dogs (Coren)
Tale of two horses – a passion for free will teaching (Gregory)
Unleashing the healing power of animals: True stories about therapy
animals – and what they do for us (Preece-Kelly)
Wildlife Garden (Kopp)
Wildlife photography from the edge (Williams)

www.hubbleandhattie.com

First published 2024 by Hubble & Hattie, an imprint of David and Charles Ltd, c/o Veloce office: 2 Poundbury Business Centre, Middle Farm Way, Poundbury, Dorchester, DT1 3WA England. Tel 01305 260068/e-mail info@veloce.co.uk.
ISBN: 978-1-787119-25-3 © Cindy-Lou Thompson & David and Charles Ltd 2024.

CONTENTS

DEDICATION & ACKNOWLEDGEMENTS

I dedicate this book to my late grandmother, Mrs Vera E Carpenter – 'Mum'. Without her love and encouragement during my formative years of all things art and dogs, my path through life would have been different. I know she would be very proud of my achievements.

A huge thank you to my loving husband, Alan, who has been right beside me through my illness, and has supported me when writing this book. He's one in a million.

Thank you to Jude and the team at Hubble & Hattie, who have worked so hard in getting my books into print.

PREFACE

I was raised by my grandmother, who I called Mum. She ran a large family business in the Bedfordshire countryside – and we lived in a 450 year old timber-framed, mud and daub thatched cottage. Mum was a very well-respected dog trainer, who ran her own competitive dog training club, and set some well-known professional dog trainers on their paths to specialised work. She bred Irish Wolfhounds, and we would compete annually at many championship and exemption shows throughout the year, always culminating with an entry or two at Crufts Dog Show, and also ran boarding kennels and trained dogs for security.

My life was very dog orientated but, being very musical and artistic as a child, I was encouraged by family and an excellent private education to indulge in art and music, and it was my love of art that allowed my creativity to grow.

Whilst I've had varied employment – security dog trainer, dog warden, laboratory technician, courier, private secretary, HGV driver, to name a few (and I also read Arabic at Leeds University) – my love of art was never far away, and I continued to sketch, paint and model animals.

Although I had already backpacked to many countries, my life really changed when I met my husband, Alan, and we decided to move into a converted van, initially, and later a truck, and do some serious independent travelling. Our first big road trip was overland to Kathmandu and back, through 18 countries; 22,366 miles in 12 months. We lived for 13 years on the road, working the summer months in the UK and travelling during the winter months around Europe, Asia and North Africa. We could have continued living this way of life, but something beckoned us to settle down and the timing couldn't have been better. I had been suffering for many years with what were to become very serious bladder/kidney plumbing issues, which became more frequent after we settled in one place, causing a number of serious sepsis infections that almost claimed my life. The situation culminated nine years later in a urostomy, which was a positive move, health-wise.

Whilst recovering from the sepsis episodes I needed something 'arty' to occupy my mind and hands, and I stumbled across needle felting by a famous Japanese artist, Kirino Mirii, who developed the art in the early 2000s in Japan, progressing to become a world class needle felter. I was very fortunate to meet Kirino Mirii in 2017 when she was part of a Japanese art exhibition in London, and was shocked to discover that she knew of me and my work!

At the time I started needle felting there were no books or videos showing how it was done, so I am rather proud of the fact that I am completely self-taught. I bought my first needles from Felt Alive in America, and bargained with a local sheep shearer for a couple of fleeces in return for some homemade marmalade and some of our eggs. I had to find out how to wash and card (brush the wool and make it fluffy) the fleece, and this gave me a good start.

With lots of practice, many disasters and growing interest from those around me, I began to develop my own style and techniques. The art of needle felting was immensely helpful during my health problems as it kept me focused, and gave me something productive to do. As I improved, more people wanted to buy my work, and I actually began selling my creations on eBay, with my first dog, a pug mix, going for £3.33. Once I broke the £100 barrier I set up my own Facebook page, website and other social media sites.

Over the years I have been needle felting – ever willing to push boundaries and make mistakes – I have developed techniques that are not found anywhere else. For example, my method of making realistic eyes, discovered by mistake, has transformed my sculptures, and given them taxidermic eyes in miniature. Discovering other art mediums that one

wouldn't usually consider mixing with wool have also made a huge difference to the finished sculptures. I shall continue to experiment, make mistakes, and develop more techniques with what is a totally addictive art form.

I'd like to introduce my little helper, at this point, my tabby cat, Monkey (aka Smonks and Punky Monkey). She loves to keep me company whilst I felt, and is sometimes very helpful, telling me to take a rest, or that she'd like to pose with my first book: *Needle Felting Dogs.*

I hope this book will help you on your journey of discovering and then improving your needle felting: whilst the book might concentrate on specific animals, the techniques shown here should prove useful for any other needle felting subject you might wish to specialise in.

Happy felting!

INTRODUCTION

I was immensely pleased to have been asked by Hubble & Hattie to write a third needle felting book, as it meant I could share even more ideas, techniques and tricks.

As with my previous books, *A Masterclass in Needle Felting Dogs* and *A Masterclass in Needle Felting Wildlife*, this book is intended for those who can confidently use a range of felting needles to felt into any shape or form and who wish to take their needle felting journey to another level, as well as those who would simply like to improve their techniques.

The subjects for this book are wild animals from around the world, which, for various reasons such as habitat destruction, hunting and other human-inflicted pressures, have become endangered, some of them critically. I have included the three mammals: Snow Leopard, Painted Dog, and Przewalski's Horse, along with the rather unusual Secretary Bird. The Snow Leopard, Painted Dog and Przewalski's Horse were popular requests amongst needle felters for this book. I decided to add the Secretary Bird for a challenge and for something completely different!

As with the other books, the techniques shown in these chapters can be transferred to many other animals and objects, and this book therefore provides useful information for any needle felter.

Explaining detailed shaping of these animals is not covered, that is left to the reader to use their own artistic interpretation and it is advised to study lots of photos of each animal from different angles to help guide their shaping and form. So apart from the detail of the armature plan, the initial covering and shaping of wool is not shown in any detail, but is instead shown when completed. This book does, however, cover the following:

- How to create an armature for differently proportioned animals and in various poses
- Two methods for creating eyes
- Method for creating noses
- Method for creating hooves and a beak
- Three methods for creating feathers
- How to prepare and blend Merino wool to achieve many more shades and hues
- Two methods for attaching Merino tops for long coat attachment
- Reverse felting a coat
- How to add extra finishing colours
- How to add texture to a Merino coat
- How to add smoothness to a very short coat
- How to make a grass and stone base from wool
- How to attach whiskers
- How to attach feathers

I urge readers to thoroughly read all the chapters of this book before attempting any of the projects, as a couple of techniques, fur attachment and blending, are written as separate chapters towards the end of the book to prevent unnecessary repetition.

I hope you have as much fun making these animals as I did creating and writing about them.

Most importantly, relax and have fun. Take your time and enjoy the journey, and don't be afraid to make mistakes. A mistake will always teach you something, even if it's only not to repeat it.

Happy felting!

GETTING STARTED: TOOLS & EQUIPMENT

You can have as many or as few tools as you like: purist needle felters like to create everything with wool, so have very few tools, but I think needle felting is an art that is open to interpretation. I have always strived to achieve a taxidermic-like finish, which demands the use of extra items. There's no right or wrong way: let your imagination run wild! Many of the items listed here can be found in a good craft store or sewing shop, while some tools can be found for next to nothing in thrift shops, and most items are available online from eBay or Amazon.

Needles
1

You will need a comprehensive set of needles to make the animals in this book. My favourites, after many years of felting, are WizPick (The Olive Sparrow, Etsy) and Felt Alive (www.feltalive.com). HeidiFeathers (www.heidifeathers.com) also offers a comprehensive range.

There are already quite a few different

2

Needle felting brush

Clover claw/mat cleaner

Multi-sprung Clover-type tool

Prym multi-needle holder

3-in-line needle holder

makes of felting needles, and I hope that, as the art grows in popularity, there will be more to choose from. You might notice that I don't mention which needle to use as I work through the chapters, and this is because what suits one person might not suit another. The very best advice I can give is to regularly try different needles from your armoury as you work, and make a note of the results. Don't forget to try them out at different angles to the wool surface, too, because very different results can be achieved with the same needle.

Needle holders and felting brush
2

Needle holders can hold up to seven needles (other holders can hold more, but I haven't had much success with these). The three-in-a-row holder is probably the one I use the most, but not for felting! I tend to use it for arranging a coat, which it does extremely well. The five-needle Prym holder is very useful for felting larger areas quickly, and I tend to fill it with HeidiFeathers 36 Regular (dark green tipped). The other Clover-type, blue, multi-needle holder

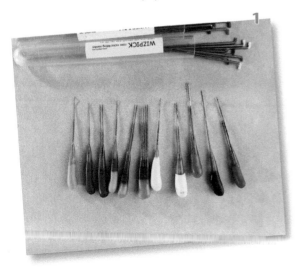

1

WIZPICK

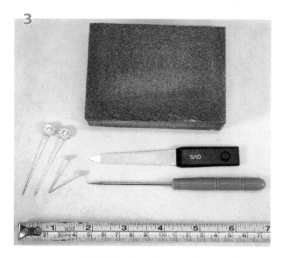

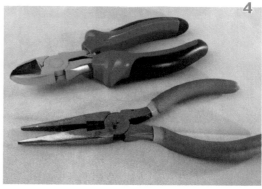

is sprung and shielded, and is perfect for felting flat items, such as ears, on a felting brush.

The felting brush is necessary for felting flat items in conjunction with the multi-sprung tool. The Clover Claw/mat cleaner is useful for cleaning your felting brush and for texturing coats.

Pins and other things

I often use long hat pins to arrange ears until I am ready to felt them into place, and they are also very useful for holding the sculpture in place on a felting sponge whilst I work. Smaller sewing pins help shape a nose: both can be found in sewing shops and online.

A sanding block and nail file (both found in pound shops) are good for sanding a nose to obtain a good surface texture, and an awl is invaluable, especially when fitting eyes and for lifting ears from a felting brush (I would be lost without one). These are readily available online or in needle felting starter kits.

A decent tape measure is essential for measuring armature and proportions to create the animals in this book. A ruler would suffice, but I use a small, retractable metal tape measure. I have also used iron-on hemming tape in both black and white to help create the feathers.

Pliers and wire cutters

You will need a decent quality pair of pliers and some wire cutters, which can be found online or your local hardware shop.

Wire

I use plastic-coated wire of 1.3mm (17 gauge) and 2mm (12 gauge) thickness, as I find the plastic coating much kinder on both needles and my fingers! I use the thicker wire for larger sculptures, and especially one with long legs that need the extra support. You will most likely find these wires in a garden centre or local hardware store, and sometimes a pound shop. They can be bought online, but tend to be a little more expensive due to shipping costs.

Scissors
6

I use a pair of Westcott four inch scissors, which are small, pointed and very sharp! With daily use for trimming coats, they last two years, on average. I also have a couple of pairs of small embroidery scissors, which are useful for those more difficult to reach parts as they have a smaller and finer point. A large pair of Westcott scissors are useful for cutting lengths of wool tops, which helps extend the life expectancy of smaller trimming scissors.

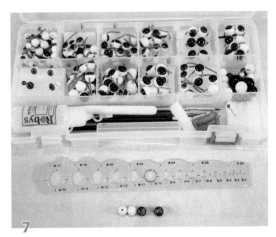

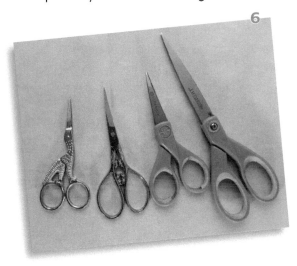

Acrylic beads and circle templates
7

For the projects in this book you will need only 8mm (0.31in) off-white or ivory acrylic beads to create the eyes, which are easily coloured using alcohol pens. These beads are very easy to fit, and there's no need to worry about the bead hole showing, as only one third of the eye is visible when in place, with the rest concealed in the eye socket. Unfortunately, beads are available in even sizes only.

To prevent beads being scratched when creating an eye socket, a set of working 'spacer beads' will be required. These can be any colour and material (though glass beads are long-lasting), as they are used only to create the perfect space for the actual eye

beads when ready to be fitted. When the eye surround is completed, simply swap the spacer beads for the finished eyes.

Circle templates are essential for colouring the beads to make the eyes. The template contains the application of colour in a perfect circle on the beads, and ensures they are both the same size: a feat impossible to achieve freehand. For ease of use, I cut this range from the template as they can be rather bulky to handle, and you won't need the other sizes for these projects.

Alcohol pens
8

There are a few makes on the market – Touch Liit, Script Twin Markers, Illustrator – but my favourite is Spectrum Noir (www. spectrumnoir.com). Originally designed for paper art, I discovered that the Spectrum Noir

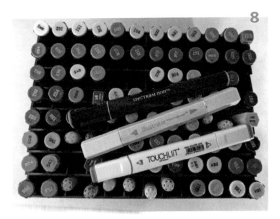

pens also colour acrylic beads; the recently created Tri-Blend has three shades of one colour in a single pen. These are essential for making eyes, and for colouring and shading wool on the finished sculpture. You can purchase these individually or in packs of similar hues. The important point is that they must be alcohol-based and not Aqua or water-based, as the alcohol colouring can then be sealed with a water-based gloss. (NOTE: Whilst Aqua markers colour the beads, the pigment is easily wiped off.)

Cabochons
9

The cabochons used in this book are transparent, flat-domed circles that can be made from epoxy resin or glass. They can be used to create the lens of an eye, and glued onto any printed or painted eyes so that these can be seen through the dome of the cabochon.

also be dampened to re-soften it to correct mistakes, and it colours well with acrylic paints or alcohol markers.

FIMO is a polymer clay that has to be baked at 110°C (230°F) to cure and harden it, and can be coloured with acrylic paints and alcohol markers. FIMO comes in a large range of colours that can be mixed to achieve different shades, and is perfect for making nails, but not so good for noses, which tend not to fit perfectly as it's necessary to bake the clay, which often alters the shape in the process.

Silk Clay is another air-drying, water-based clay that, when cured, has a slight rubber-like texture. Used in small quantities, it cures quickly, but can be dampened with water to keep it pliable. Silk clay is perfect for creating eyelids.

Clays
10

I have used three different clays in this book. Air-drying, water-based clay such as DAS and Claydium can be moulded and simply left to dry and cure. The especially useful quality of this type of clay is that the moulding can be done on the sculpture, and oven baking is not needed to harden the moulding. The clay can

Modelling tools
11

A comprehensive range of clay modelling tools exists – ball tools, flat tools, etc, of different sizes – and can be made from metal, plastic or wood. I particularly like the rubber-tipped tools for working on eyelids, as they mould around the eye with ease without damaging it: the horseshoe-shaped end is perfect for eyes; you should find one of these in a small-sized set.

Smaller-ended tools are perfect for the projects in this book, shown for size next to a tape measure. A range of both clay modelling or cake decorating tools can be utilised.

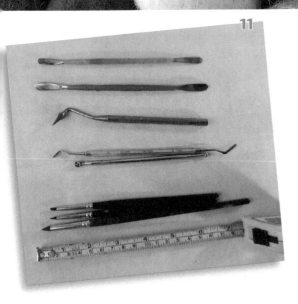

11

13

Glossy Accents™

12

This is a clear, water-based sealant that adds a three-dimensional, glass-like finish to eyes. There are other makes, but ensure they are water-based so that the sealant can be safely used over the alcohol colouring without making the colours run. Readily available in card-making shops and online, it is often referred to as Diamond Glaze.

eye of any dust or stray wool before applying finishing gloss sealer.

Mod Podge™

14

A wonderful range of sealants/glues, that can be used for a variety of jobs, from simply gluing to texturing fur, stiffening the insides of ears to make them retain a certain position, and finishing off glossy mouth parts, noses, and nails. I regularly use matt, silk and gloss versions.

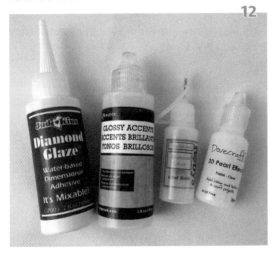

12

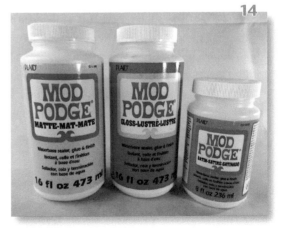

14

Paintbrushes

13

A good selection of paintbrushes is useful, and particularly nail art brushes, which are very fine and pointed, and perfect for applying Pan Pastels. I often use a thick brush to clean the

Pan Pastels

15

These are a brand of soft pastel that can be used like paint and applied with a brush. Whilst expensive, they will last forever as they have excellent coverage and a strong pigment.

15

I started off with the Drawing Set, a ten-colour selection of natural browns, greys and whites, including a black. There are 92 colours in the Pan Pastel range in total, and I have purchased a few extra to add to my collection. I have had my Pan Pastels for over two years now, and have used them on every sculpture, though haven't even made a dent in them! If you don't want the expense of Pan Pastels, ordinary pastels are okay, although the pigment isn't as strong.

Mini iron and hair straighteners
16

A mini iron – also called a Wax Master Kit – has many uses, such as fabric distressing, wax art, gem embellishing, mini iron and pyrography. I found it very useful for smoothing felted surfaces, especially on legs and faces. Various tips can be purchased to give different finishes. Hair straighteners (small size) are perfect for

16

flattening and shaping ears, although an iron on a wool setting can be used instead.

Wool
17, 18

A quick note about the wool used for these projects. There are essentially two types of industrial processed wool, the first of which is core wool. Sometimes called batts, this is wool that has been washed and carded, resulting in a fluffy mass of naturally curly or wavy fibres that have become entangled. It is very easy to felt and create almost any shape with this wool.

Core wool can also come in slivers that, instead of a large fluffy mass, is a long length of processed wool coiled into a ball, and is ideal for wrapping. Core wool can be dyed a range of colours.

Tops (sometimes called roving) is core wool that has been put through another process where it is, in effect, combed and stretched to make the fibres long and straight, and aligned with each other. It is usually sold in a continuous thick length of wool around 2 or 3cm (0.78in to 1.18in) thick, and looks a bit like hair. Almost any type of wool can be processed into tops, but the Merino range is by far the most popular, and can be dyed many colours. The really magical quality of Merino tops is that the different colours can be blended with carders to give a huge palette of shades and hues.

Carders are special hand-held wool devices with metal teeth, which are used as a pair to prepare or blend Merino wool, or any tops for a top coat. You simply brush the wool from one carder to another, until fluffed up and blended (small, metal-toothed dog brushes work just as well). Good needle felting outlets sell felting wool and carders, though they can also be found online.

General points
This book assumes that you, dear reader, have

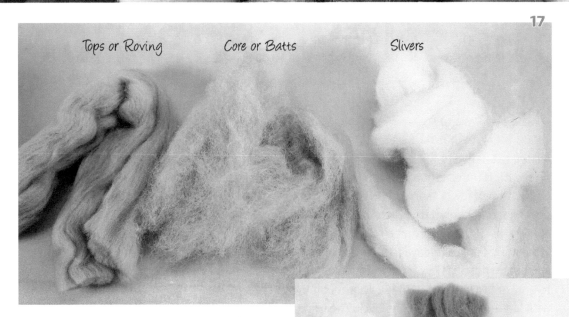

Tops or Roving   Core or Batts   Slivers

17

18

good basic knowledge of needle felting; how to use a felting needle, and how to add wool to create and maintain shaping, and that you can interpret where form needs to be added. Describing how to make a very complicated, three-dimensional shape, such as a head, would sound very clumsy, so the interpretation of shaping is encouraged and left to the sculptor, where he or she can use their own style.

Throughout the book are tips, tricks and short cuts to help overcome common issues you may encounter, as well as advise short cuts. I urge you to read the book right through before attempting any of the animals.

Invest in a good range of needles from different manufacturers, and keep trying out different ones as you work. You will soon discover your favourites. Remember also that you can experiment with your multi-holders by fitting different grade needles.

Last of all, needle felting should be a very

relaxing art form. If you are breaking needles, then you are most probably too tense. Relax and keep your touch light and gentle so that you can 'feel' where you are going and what you are creating. There is no need to be heavy-handed or to stab very quickly. If you are using the optimum grade needle for the task in hand, you will find that you can achieve excellent results, felting slowly and with purpose.

Let's get going!

THE SNOW LEOPARD

THE SNOW LEOPARD (*Panthera unica*)

A large cat native to the mountain ranges of Central and South Asia, it is listed as vulnerable on the IUCN (International Union for Conservation of Nature) Red List with a global population of fewer than 10,000 mature individuals. Their decline has been attributed to poaching and habitat destruction. They inhabit alpine and subalpine zones at elevations of 3000m to 4500m, and can be found in western China, Mongolia, and southern Siberia to the Tibetan Plateau, Himalayas and Afghanistan. They feed on wild goats, sheep, boar and other smaller mammals. They have a very thick, weather protective coat that ranges from off-white to grey or brown/grey, with black spots on the outer side of the legs, top of the tail and head, with larger rosettes along the back. The tail is usually long and bushy and their feet are large for their body size.

1

1

The instructions for the first animal in this series explain the initial making of an armature. Subsequent chapters will not repeat how to form the armature, applying the first covering of wool, or how to colour the eyes unless a different colour or method is used. Instead, only wire lengths and armature plan, with a few photos showing the base sculpture will be included. The initial methods used in this chapter will be the same for all animals. Creating this Snow Leopard will showcase a standing pose, sculpture preparation for long fur attachment, long fur blending, long fur attachment, and fur colouring, texturing and detailing once attached. It will also cover other details such as furry paws, and making realistic cabochon eyes.

The completed Snow Leopard weighs 217g (7.65oz).

ITEMS NEEDED
Core wool
- Core wool (any natural white) (World of Wool White Corriedale Slivers) 150g (5.29oz)

Merino wool
- Merino Tops, (fawn) 50g (1.7oz) (Adelaide Walker Sand)
- Merino Tops (off white) 50g (1.7oz) (World of Wool Pearl)
- Merino Tops (grey) 60g (2.11oz) (World of Wool Ash)
- Merino Tops (very dark grey) 30g (1.05oz) (World of Wool Granite)
- Merino Tops (black) 30g (1.05oz) (World of Wool Raven)
- Merino Tops (light pink) 5g (0.17oz) (World of Wool Candy Floss)

Other items
- Wire 2mm (12 gauge) 64cm (25.2in) x 1, 45cm (17.7in) x 2
- Pair of 10mm (0.39in) cabochons (the flatter type, not the high-domed type)
- Clear fishing line (rating of 2lb should be fine enough)
- Digitally painted Snow Leopard eye pdf from www.chicktincreations.com (see Method)
- Glossy Accents

TOOLS
- A comprehensive range of felting needles, including three-in-a-row, multi-sprung, multi un-sprung
- Tape measure
- Pliers and wire cutters (pointed end type)
- Awl
- Felting sponge
- Felting brush
- Scissors (small pointed)
- Long hat pins x 6
- Brushes, any small brushes
- Small pair of wire-toothed carders
- Alcohol pens, Spectrum Noir Black, GB8 and EB8
- Mod Podge Gloss and small spray bottle
- Hair straighteners/iron
- Pan pastels: Raw Umber 780.5, Titanium White 100.5, Black 800.5
- Colour printer and 4 x 6in glossy photo paper
- Small bikini shaver (optional)
- Fawn cotton and sewing needle

METHOD
Firstly, download the Snow Leopard eyes pdf from www.chicktincreations.com/Downloads for 3rd Book; enter the password SBFF. Print on 6 x 4in glossy photographic paper (paper size is essential, so that eyes will be the correct size).

Step 1
2

Measure out your three lengths of wire; 64cm (25.2in) x 1, 45cm (17.7in) x 2.

You will need to trim these once your armature has been formed, but it's always better to allow extra wire than too little, as it is easier to cut off than to add. The 69cm (27.16in) length of wire will create the tail, back, neck and head. Bend to proportions shown starting with the tail and working forwards towards the head. The other two lengths of wire are folded in half. They will be the legs.

Step 2
3

To attach the legs to the armature, take one folded-in-half wire and place it over the shoulders at the bend where the body finishes and the neck starts. Holding the body wire

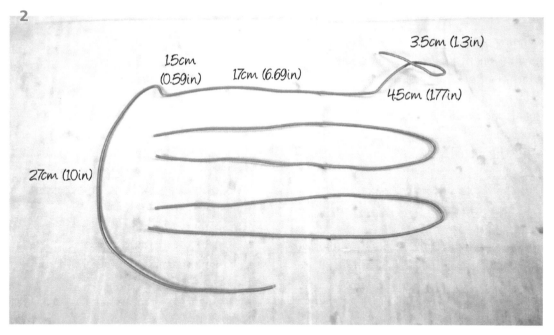

2

3.5cm (1.3in)

1.5cm (0.59in) 17cm (6.69in)

4.5cm (1.77in)

27cm (10in)

3

Wrap tightly twice around the body

Do the same for the back legs

Front legs

along with one side of the leg wire in one hand, using your other hand wrap very tightly the other side of the wire length around the body at least twice, to form a tight join and bring both wires together. Attach the back legs in the same way at the hips, where the body ends and the tail begins. They will look long and out of proportion to start with, but they will be correct at the end. If your wire wrapping is a little loose, you can nip it tighter with your pliers. Once your initial covering of wool is in place and felted tightly, your armature should stabilise.

Step 3

4

Now you have the armature wires joined, you will need to form the legs. Hold each pair of legs together and, starting at the body, bend both wires together to the measurements given in the armature plan. Bending them

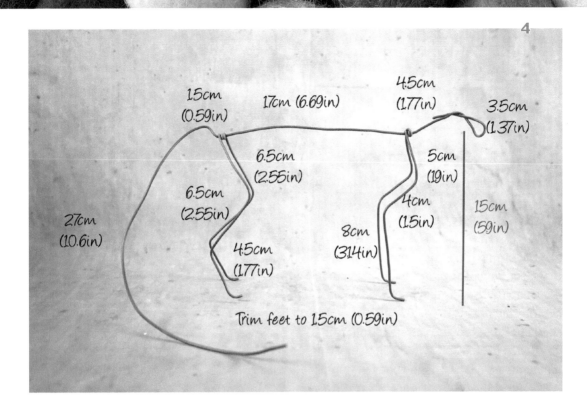

4

1.5cm (0.59in)

17cm (6.69in)

4.5cm (1.77in)

3.5cm (1.37in)

6.5cm (2.55in)

5cm (19in)

6.5cm (2.55in)

4cm (1.5in)

15cm (59in)

27cm (10.6in)

8cm (3.14in)

4.5cm (1.77in)

Trim feet to 1.5cm (0.59in)

together equally will ensure they are both the same shape and bent to the same measurements. Trim the feet to 1.5cm (0.59in). Arrange your Leopard so that he can stand squarely unaided.

Step 4
5

Using your white core wool, start the initial covering by wrapping around the neck, shoulders and working your way down the body, at least once under the tail and back onto the body again. You will have to do this in a couple of stages. Felt the wrappings tightly, then wrap thinner lengths of white core down the legs, making sure the wrapping isn't too thick at this stage, but if using Slivers, wrap a length of Sliver (roughly twice the length of a leg) split in half, down each leg. Do this by securing one end of the length of Slivers, by felting it to the body, wrap down the leg to the foot, holding the wrapping tightly, use your pliers to fold half of the foot wire back onto the wool you have wrapped, and nip tight. This

should now hold the wrapping in place, so that you can finish off and wrap the remaining length back up the leg to the body. If using core wool, ensure the wrapping is no thicker than 1.5cm (0.59in). The first wrapping is the most important, as it will not only stabilise the armature, but will provide a good base for further additions of wool.

NOTE: When wrapping, be aware that there should be enough length to wrap down and back up each leg, so keep this in mind as you wrap. Cover the other legs in the same way using an approximate 30cm (11.8in) even length of wool. Also cover the tail using the

5

same method using a length of wool almost twice the length of the tail. You should now have all the armature covered in wool, except the head.

Step 5
6, 7

Now, using your own judgement, add more white core wool to finalise the body shape of your Leopard. As you do this, decide on its final pose and take care to ensure that pose remains as you work. Take your time with this and ensure you have a fairly firm finish to the body and that you are happy with the final shaping. Use lots of photos to assess the shaping and pose you would like, and regularly check that your Leopard can stand square and unaided in the final pose you wish to replicate. When you are happy with the body shape, take a short length of core, not longer than 20cm (7.87in) and roll it up to begin the head. Felt a head shape that is no longer than 6cm (2.3in) from the back of the head to the tip of the nose. As you work on the detailing of the head, you will experience head shrinkage, so be aware of this, adding more if needed. Create indented placements for each eye (which are forward facing) that will accept each cabochon, and narrow down the muzzle and felt rough lines where the nose and mouth will be placed.

Step 6
8, 9, 10

Before going any further, read the chapter on how to prepare and blend Merino wool (page 101) to achieve different colours. Before we can add any colouring to the head, we will first have to blend some Merino wool. I tend not to use single colours, as they end up looking rather flat in colour and detail. The three blends I have made for this Snow Leopard are as follows:

Blend 1 = Sand x 1, Ash x 1
Blend 2 = Sand x 1, Pearl x 2
Blend 3 = Raven x 4, Ash x 1

Create a good amount of Blend 1 as this is the main colour of the body of the Leopard, Blend 2 is for the legs and the lower sides of the body and sides of the neck, and Blend 3 is for the dark rosettes and spots of the coat pattern and paw pads. If you didn't want to colour the coat with markers, you will need to ensure you have enough of Blend 3, otherwise, you will only need a small amount for the pads. Don't let your blends run out, as you will need to ensure a good match when you blend more. Where Blends 1 and 2 meet you will need to use equal amounts of both blends so that it gives the coat a nice gradation of colouring. Pearl is for the underbelly, chest and front of the neck and chin. You will also need to create a gradation between Blend 2 and Pearl.

Step 7
11, 12

You should now be left with three blends and some carded Pearl. Here is a colour sketch of the Snow Leopard markings and placement of blends.

Step 8
13, 14, 15

To make the eyes, first use your cabochons to help create some good eye sockets on the head, making sure they are level with each other and both looking forward and in the same direction. When you are happy with the eye placement, decide which pair of printed eyes you are going to use. Add a small amount of Glossy Accents to each eye, place a cabochon on to each eye and gently press into place to expel any bubbles and ensure a good contact. Once dried, cut out each eye and place into the eye sockets, then create some eyelids from Blend 1 to hold the cabochons in place. You can glue them if you

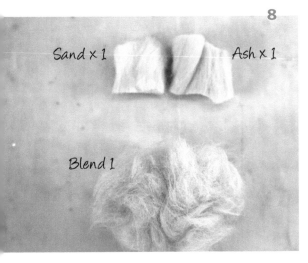

8

Sand x 1 — Ash x 1

Blend 1

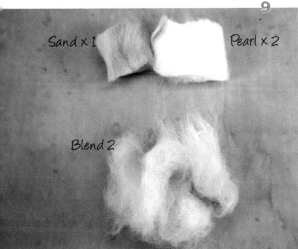

9

Sand x 1 — Pearl x 2

Blend 2

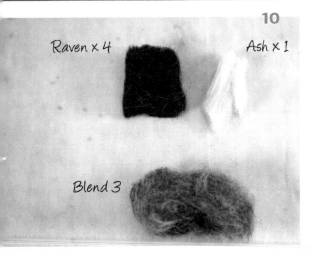

10

Raven x 4 — Ash x 1

Blend 3

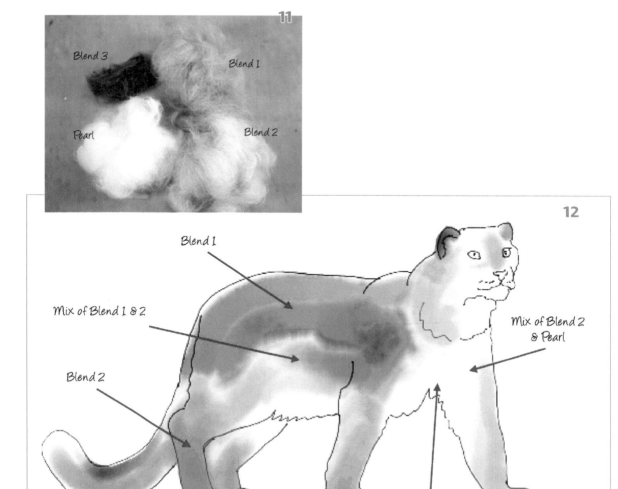

11

Blend 3   Blend 1

Pearl   Blend 2

12

Blend 1

Mix of Blend 1 & 2

Blend 2

Mix of Blend 2 & Pearl

Pearl

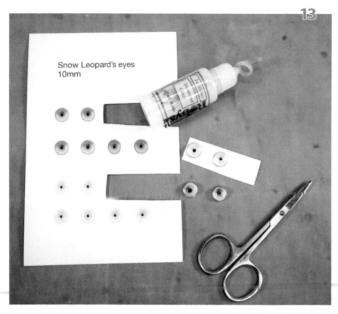

13

Snow Leopard's eyes 10mm

like, but you shouldn't need to if you create some good eyelids. As you do this, give the head an initial covering of Blend 1 over the top of the head, around the eyes, down the top of the nose and both sides of the head, leaving the chin and underside of the head white. This will be covered with Pearl later. You can also add some detailing of the nose and mouth with Blend 3 and a little Candy Floss to colour the nose. Continue adding more detail to the head, ensuring the length of the head remains around 5.5cm (2.1in).

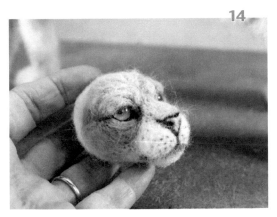

14

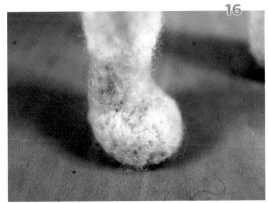

16

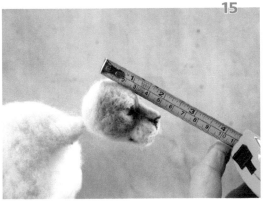

15

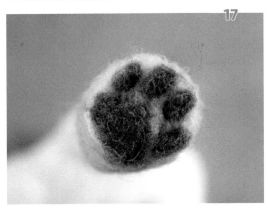

17

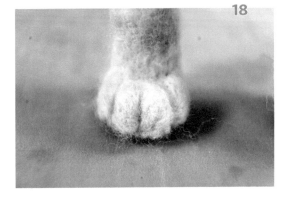

18

Step 9
16, 17, 18

For the feet, give them a covering of Blend 2 creating an overall shaping of the foot. Snow Leopards have big round-shaped feet that are very large for the size of their bodies! Felt on some pads with Blend 3. To create the toes, make three cuts into each foot, using the pads as a guide. Make the cuts on the top of each foot, rather than on the underside of the foot. Felt into the cuts to round off each toe to give them shape. As the Snow Leopard is going to be standing on some snow, you don't have to create the pads, but it is good practice to do so.

Step 10
19, 20

See the chapter on fur attachment, which shows how to add long fur. For the coat pattern, you can use a couple of different methods. The first method, which I used for the front legs, is to use a black alcohol marker to mark out the pattern on the body and, as you attach the Merino long fur, use these markers as a guide. I find this a rather fiddly method, which doesn't always turn out as detailed as you might expect, as you have to be very particular when adding the darker fur to the rosette markings, ensuring you cover the markings very accurately. You also have to be aware of adding a good coverage of the main coat colour whilst taking note of where the two main colours (the white under

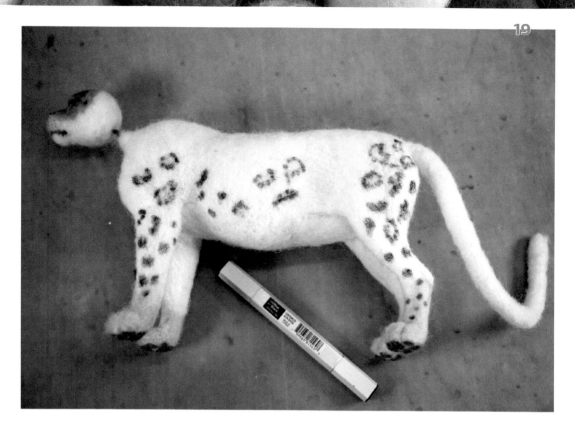

body and darker upper body) meet. Rushing this step can leave you with gaps around the darker markings.

I started the front legs with this first method then changed to the marker method as described in Step 11 for the back legs.

Step 11
21, 22, 23

The second method, which I find a lot easier, is to add the main colouring of Merino long fur (minus the rosettes and spots) to the body, then use an alcohol marker to colour the fur. Start covering the body with your Merino blends, using the body colouring diagram shown in Step 7. Make sure you have a good thick coverage of fur, by adding your long fur attachments very close together and not leaving any gaps. When you have created a good thick covering of fur over the body, arrange the fur using a three-in-

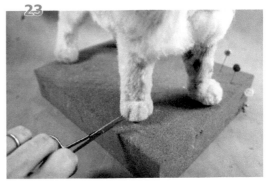

line needle tool, so that it is ready to have a first trim. You will need to do a couple more trims to add shaping. You can use your small pointed scissors to do this, or a small bikini-type shaver. Mine was brand new and broke during this process! So I only managed to give the Leopard one good shaving. Add a good covering over the feet and legs and define the toes again by felting a groove between each toe, which should be easy to find as they are already shaped.

Step 12
24, 25, 26

Now for the fun part, if you are using the alcohol markers to colour the coat! Start

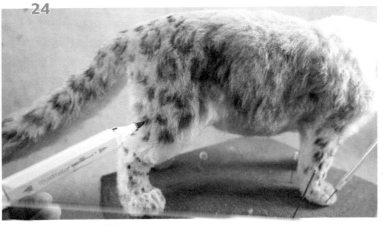

25

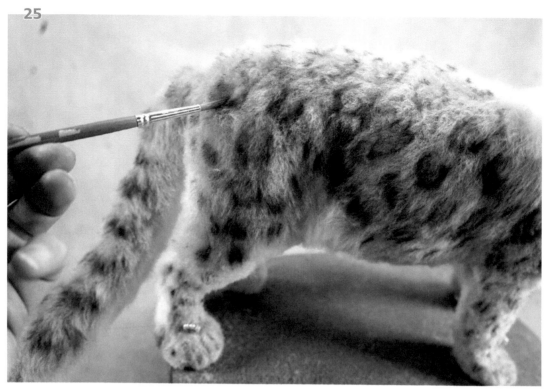

26

TIP: The coat markings are equal and regular for both sides, so plan and work systematically, starting along the back and tail, then spreading down on each side, marking a rosette one side, then in the same place on the other side and so on. You can pin all four feet of the Leopard to your felting sponge using long hat pins, to minimise handing.

Step 13
27, 28, 29

marking the rosettes over the body. The rosettes tend to be on the larger main areas of the body and the spots on the smaller parts, such as legs and neck. To lightly colour inside of the rosettes, using a small, soft paint brush, apply some Pan Pastel Raw Umber 780.1. You might find you will need to apply these colours a couple of times, to ensure an even and deep colouring. Use your black alcohol marker to add the coat pattern to the head.

To create the ears, using a felting brush and a multi-sprung needle tool, felt a couple of ears with some Merino Raven to the shape and dimensions shown. Felt them to a thickness of around 2mm (0.07in), leaving the bottom edge of each ear unfelted to aid attachment to the head. You will also need to create a couple of white patches on the back of the Snow Leopard's ears using some Merino Pearl. When shaping the ears, ensure you keep a clear left and right. The inside length of each ear is shorter than the outside length. When you have felted, shaped and trimmed each ear, felt the white patches in the centre of the back of each ear. Felt them into place from the BACK of the ear only. This will prevent any black wool being pushed through and into the white. Lift the ears off using an awl regularly as you felt. When you have finished, flatten each ear using an iron on the wool setting, or use some hair straighteners.

Step 14

30

Turn the ears over, so that the inside of each ear is facing upwards, and felt on a long fur covering of Blend 1 to the inside of both ears as you did for the coat, so that it resembles fur. Attach this wool carefully, making sure you don't push right through to the other side, but only inside the thickness of each ear. This can be achieved by felting along and into the ear, rather than straight down and through it. Trim the attached wool to the shape of the ears.

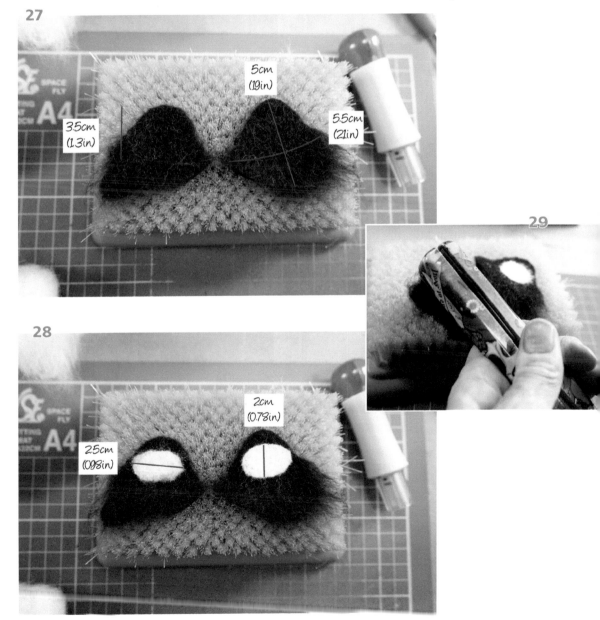

30

Step 15

31

Attach each ear to the head. You can use long hat pins to help with this, to hold them in place as you assess their position and felt into place. They might look a little large at this point, but some more fur will be added around the head, which will make them appear smaller.

31

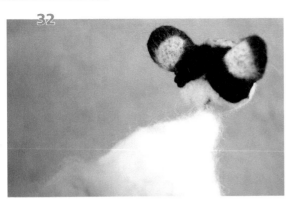

Step 16
32, 33, 34

Place the head on the body and felt a neck to secure it in place. Continue adding long fur to cover the neck and head around the front of the ears, making sure you follow the fur colour pattern shown in Step 7. Trim the fur when done, and tidy up any pattern work.

35

Step 17
35, 36

Finish off the markings around the neck and head and give the fur another trim. You should now have a Snow Leopard that looks something like this. A final trim is still needed, so don't be tempted to trim off too much at this stage.

36

Step 18
37, 38, 39

To create a snow base, using some core white wool, a felting brush and a multi-sprung needle tool, felt a flat shape that is large enough to accommodate the standing leopard and his tail. Felt the main shape flat and firm for both sides, then add a very loose fluffy layer of white core to simulate some snow, making sure you leave some space for his feet to be placed. With your base completed, it should look something like this. We will sew the Leopard to the base later.

37

38

39

Step 19
40, 41, 42, 43

When you are happy with the coat and markings and the trim, you can now texture the coat to make it more durable and less liable to be damaged if touched. Thoroughly mix one part Mod Podge Gloss to five parts water and put into a little spray bottle. Give

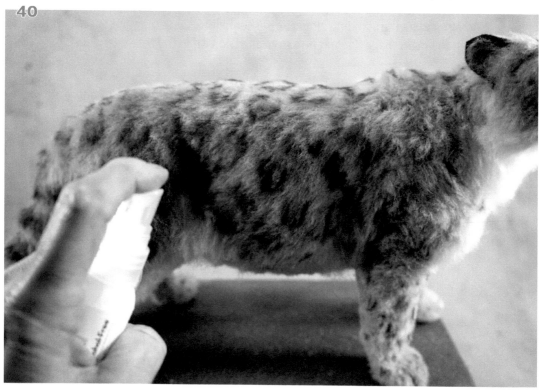

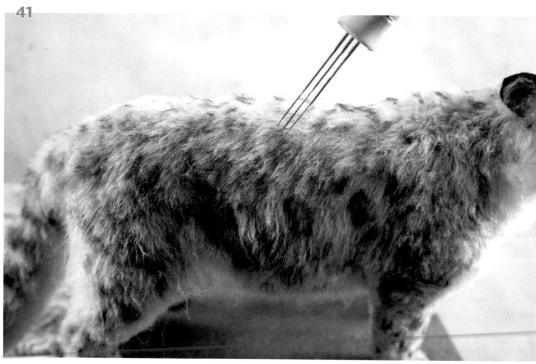

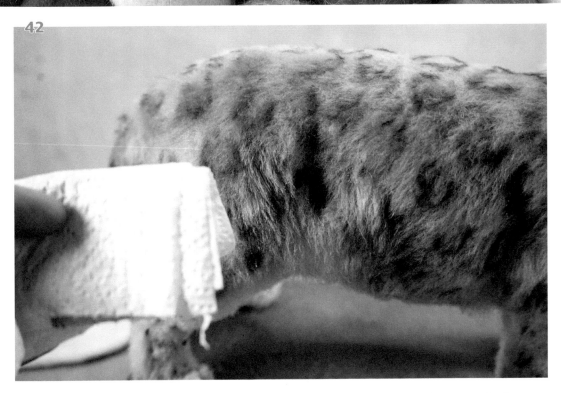

42

the Leopard a spray of the mixture in sections and using a three-in-line needle tool, arrange the fur in the direction you want it and allow to dry. If you have sprayed too much of the mixture, simply dab the affected area with a piece of kitchen towel and continue to arrange the fur. Allow to dry and redo any parts that

need it. You will also need to give a final trim and tidy up of the coat. When doing this, observe that Snow Leopards have varying lengths of fur on different parts of their body. For example, they have slightly longer fur on the lower back part of their legs up to the hock joint, and shorter fur at the front.

43

44

45

Step 20
44, 45, 46

Using a needle and some light clear fishing line, thread some whiskers through the muzzle, making a loose knot at the end of the fishing line, so that when it is pulled through the muzzle, the knot will be large enough to resist being pulled out easily the other side. Trim to length and repeat to make at least six whiskers on each side.

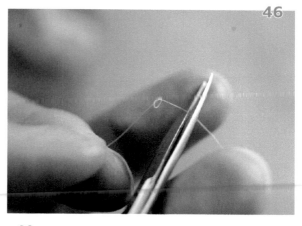

46

Step 21
47, 48

Finally, attach the feet onto the snow base by sewing a couple of stitches with some fawn coloured thread, through each foot and the base and tying a knot underneath the base to secure ... and you're done!

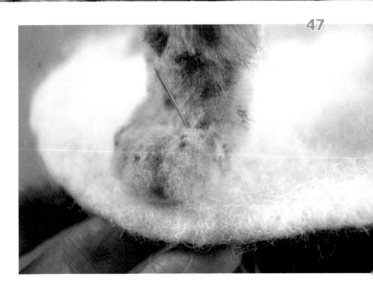

PRZEWALSKI'S HORSE

PRZEWALSKI'S HORSE (*Equus ferus przewalskii*)
(Pronounced sheh-VAL-ski) AKA Mongolian Wild Horse

A rare wild horse, originally native to the Steppes of Central Asia, Przewalski's Horse is also known as the Takhi, Mongolian Wild Horse and Dzungarian Horse. It is considered the only truly 'wild' horse, as opposed to feral horses. It is a strong and stocky animal with a typical height of 12-14 hands, and is most commonly Dunn in colour with black extremities, mane and tail. The mane is unusual and stands upright. In 2011, an estimated 400 horses existed in the wild, but with the help of captive bred ones being re-introduced into protected reserves in China, Kazakhstan and Russia, this number slowly increased to around 2000. Numbers had suffered due to changes in land use, military activities, poaching for food, and hard winters. These horses really were brought back from the edge of extinction!

1

1

The methods for the second animal in this series, a Przewalski's Horse, show how to create hooves and demonstrate reverse needle felting. This model is suitable for those who struggle with long fur attachment, as the only long fur to attach in this sculpture is the mane and tail, and is the easiest to create in this book.

The completed Przewalski's Horse weighs 117g (4.12oz).

ITEMS NEEDED
Core wool
- Core wool Natural White (any suitable white as it will be covered) 60g (2.11oz)
- Core wool Carded Batts Biscuit 60g (2.11oz) (Wingham Wool)
- Core wool Carded Batts Caramel 30g (1.05oz) (Wingham Wool)
- Core wool Carded Shetland Natural Grey Batt 35g (1.23oz) (World of Wool)
- Core wool Corriedale Slivers Raven 30g (1.05oz) (World of Wool)

Merino wool (for the mane and tail)
- Merino Tops, Raven 20g (0.7oz) (World of Wool)
- Merino Tops Sand 10g (0.35oz) (Wingham Wool)

Other items
- Wire 2mm (12 gauge) 47cm (18.5in), 45cm (17.7in) x 2
- White or off-white 8mm (0.31in) acrylic beads x 2
- Another pair of beads the same size to use as 'spacer' beads, so your final eyes are not scratched. Any colour glass beads will do.

TOOLS
- A comprehensive range of felting needles, including three-in-a-row, multi-sprung, multi unsprung
- Tape measure
- Pliers and wire cutters (pointed end type)
- Awl
- Black thread and sewing needle
- Plastic circle template with 6mm (0.23in) circle
- Silk Clay Black
- Clay tools. Set of small soft-ended, pointed and horseshoe shaped
- Nail file and cheap nail art filing block with different grades of filing paper
- Felting sponge
- Felting brush
- Scissors (small pointed)

- Self-closing tweezers
- Long hat pins x 6
- Brushes, any narrow 'nail art' brushes, 3mm (0.11in) and 12mm (0.47in)
- Small pair of wire-toothed carders
- Alcohol pens, Spectrum Noir Black, EB8
- Diamond Glaze clear
- Clear drying craft glue (not super-glue or UHU)
- Mod Podge Gloss and Matt, plus small spray bottle
- Kitchen towel
- Hair straighteners/iron
- Quilting iron/pyrography hot foil tool
- Pan Pastels: Raw Umber 780.5, Raw Umber Ex Dark 780.1, Neutral Grey 820.5, Black 800.5

METHOD
Step 1
2

Measure out your three lengths of wire: 47cm (18.5in), and 45cm (17.7in) x 2, using the longest length to make the tail, back, neck and head. Fold the remaining two lengths in half to make the legs and attach them to the body to create your armature to the measurements shown. Bend the legs to length and curl under the ends of each leg as shown, making sure the armature can stand evenly with all four legs on a flat surface and trim any excess wire. The hooves will be attached to these.

Step 2
3, 4, 5

Cover the armature with the white core wool, and build up some shaping and rough detail of the shoulders and back legs. Build up the bottom half of the legs with some core Raven so that they are half covered with white and half covered with Raven. Take note of where

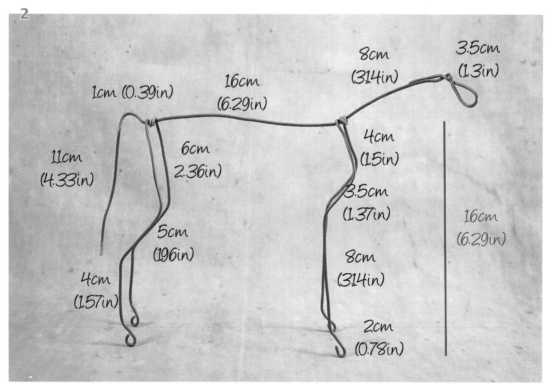

2

1cm (0.39in)

16cm
(6.29in)

8cm
(3.14in)

3.5cm
(1.3in)

11cm
(4.33in)

6cm
2.36in)

4cm
(1.5in)

3.5cm
(1.37in)

16cm
(6.29in)

5cm
(1.96in)

4cm
(1.57in)

8cm
(3.14in)

2cm
(0.78in)

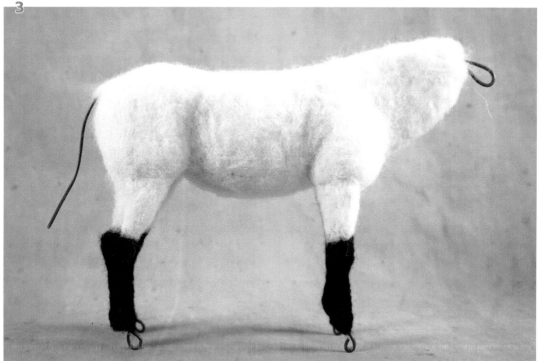

3

the black colouring of the legs finishes. You will need it to be a little below where you finally want the markings to end, as we are going to colour the gradation in later.

Step 3
06, 07

Now you have some form to your Horse, you will need to add some colour. For the

4

5

6

Raven   Caramel   Biscuit

underside and inside of the top half of the legs, use Caramel, and for the remainder of the body down to the Raven on the legs, use Biscuit. Use these colours to create more detailing of muscle and form. Take some time over this and study lots of photos. Overlap the Caramel and Biscuit to make the colours blend, though we will be refining this later.

from the back of the head to the tip of the nose. Allow for some shrinkage as you work on the detailing and add as necessary. Felt some nostrils and a line where the mouth will be placed. Once you have the basic shape of the head, cover with some Biscuit, leaving the nose area free showing the Caramel. Once you are happy with your head shaping, cut a horizontal

Step 4
08, 09, 10, 11

Using some Caramel, create a basic shaped horse head that will measure 6.5cm (2.55in)

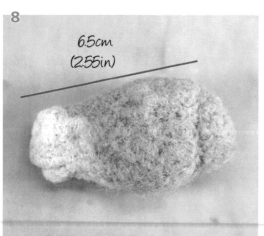

6.5cm
(2.55in)

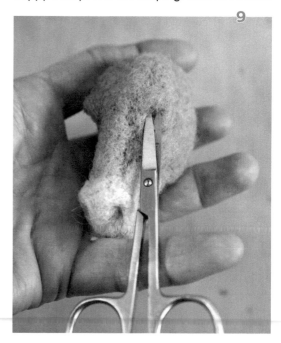

opening for each eye, (in-keeping with how a natural eye would open and close) enough to accept a couple of 8mm (0.31in) spacer beads. These beads should sit far enough inside the head, so that only a third of the bead is showing. Use the spacer beads to help you build up good shaping around the eyes. When you are ready to fit the final eyes, these beads should easily pop out and swap with the finished eyes. Cut a channel into the base of the head (shown by red arrow) so that it can fit onto the neck wire, and see how it looks for size. Adjust the wire as needed to make a correct length of neck.

Step 5
12, 13

To make the final eyes, place one of the acrylic beads onto the end of an awl, to hold it steady. Using an alcohol pen EB8 and a circle template of 6mm (0.23in), place and press the

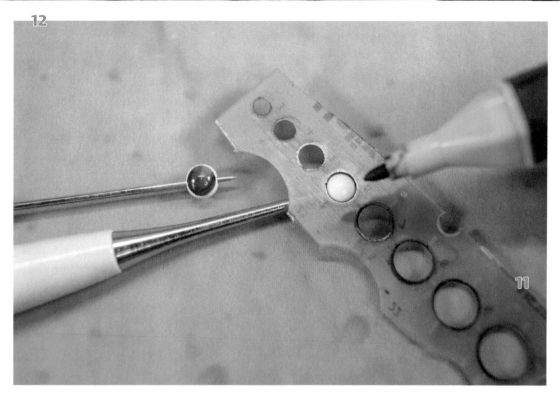

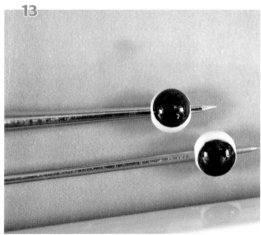

pen, make an oval-shaped pupil with rounded ends in the centre of each eye, using a dotting method, which is much easier to do than drawing the shape. Build up the pupil shape by placing black dots onto the bead. Around the pupil, place some more EB8 colouring by dotting around the edge of the pupil and outward over the iris. You should be left with a nice dark coloured horse eye, which has a very natural colouring. Give another coating of Diamond Glaze and allow to dry. Add more detail if you wish after the Diamond Glaze has dried, then add another coat of glaze.

Step 6
14, 15

Whilst the eyes are drying, make the hooves. Using some Shetland Natural Grey, felt some hoof shapes. Felt these as solidly as you can. Don't fret too much about getting an ultra smooth surface, as you can trim the surface smooth with scissors. It's more important to get the overall shape right. The back hooves are slightly more upright than the front

template tightly onto the bead and colour inside the circle with the EB8 pen. In one definite circular motion, give the bead a good colouring, then remove the template and leave to dry (if you keep adding markings to the eye as it dries, you will remove the colour you have just added). When dried, give it a coating of Diamond Glaze, using a damp nail art brush. Leave to dry. (This is to allow touch up colouring, without removing what you have already done.) Using the black alcohol

14

Back   Front

15

them a coat of Mod Podge Matt. You will need to cover only the trimmed surfaces (not the top couple of millimetres, as this will be needed to felt the hoof to the leg). You will need to do this in a couple of stages; some self-closing tweezers will help with this stage, and some long hat pins to secure them to a felting sponge to dry. So, do the hoof walls first, then, once that covering has dried, the underside of the hooves. When the hooves have dried, using a nail file, give the glued surfaces a filing, to smooth them down. Picture 17 shows the difference between a filed hoof and a non-filed hoof. With the filing completed, give each hoof another generous covering of Mod Podge Matt. Allow to dry and repeat the filing another couple of times. You can finish off the filing with a nail art filing block to give a shinier surface. You will have created some nice realistic hooves.

hooves. Create four hooves and cut an opening large enough into which the bent wires can be placed. Designate one hoof to a particular leg and keep them in that order. You might have to fiddle around with them to ensure they fit on the ends of the legs and that the horse can stand squarely on a flat surface. Adjust the bend of the wires if needed.

> TIP: Use some long pins to pin your hooves in order on your felting sponge, so they don't get knocked or misplaced.

Step 7
16, 17, 18
Keeping your hooves in foot order, give them a close surface trim to remove any fuzziness, on every surface except a couple of millimetres along the top part of each hoof. Then give

16

17

Glued & Filed

Glued

Red lines indicate where the glue application stops.

18

Smooth

Shine

Step 9
19, 20

With the hooves completely dried, slot the respective feet wires into each hoof to check the correct hoof is on the correct leg. Then one at a time using some Core Raven, loosely wrap the exposed wire, down onto the top of the hoof so that it slightly overlaps the hoof, and felt them into place. Do this by felting down into the hoof and build up the pastern shape on the legs. When finished, the hoof should look as though it is growing from the

19

20

leg naturally and the top line of unglued hoof, will aid this step. No glue is needed and is why the top surface of each hoof is left uncovered with Mod Podge, to allow the easy attachment of wool.

Step 10

21

Add some more colouring and detail to the nose by colouring it with some Pan Pastels. I have used a range of greys, making the colouring darker on the end of the nose and

21

lighter as you work back to the muzzle. You can also add a little black to the inside of the nostrils and mouth, to add some depth, and a little white to add highlighting. Remove the spacer beads, give the eyelids a trim, and fit your finished eyes. Check they are a good fit, and that the wool sockets are the correct size and they don't show any whites of the eyes.

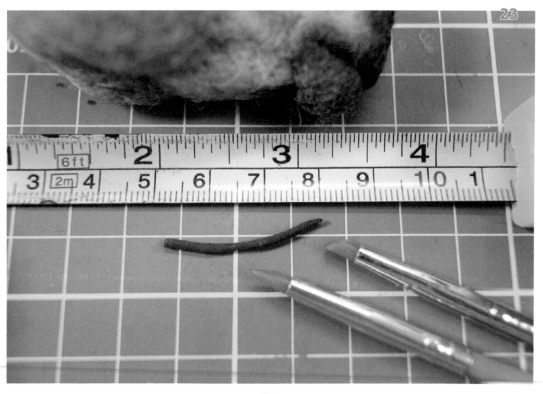

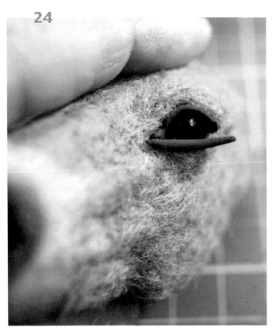

24

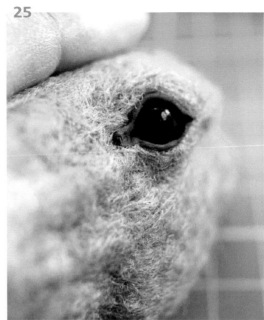

25

When you are happy with the fit, remove them and add a small dab of any craft glue deep inside each socket and replace the eyes. Be sure to move them into the right position before the glue dries. Make sure the glue is set completely before moving to the next step. Trim any stray lengths of wool away from the eyes.

Step 11
22, 23, 24, 25

To complete the eyelids, you will need some Mod Podge Gloss, black Silk Clay, some small silicone tipped clay modelling tools, (especially the one with a horseshoe-shaped tip) small scissors and a paint brush; also some water, a surface to roll the clay and some kitchen towel. You will need to do these steps rather quickly, to prevent the Mod Podge and Silk Clay from drying too quickly as you work. Work on one eye at a time. Have everything ready, then give the eye and inner eyelid a coat of Mod Podge Gloss using a damp brush. This is where you are going to stick the clay eyelid. Roll out a thin length of Silk Clay that is no more than 2mm (0.07in) and at least 2cm (0.78in) in length, long enough to fix to either

the top half of the eye or the bottom half (don't attempt to do the eye all in one length, as this will get messy). Apply the end of a length to one corner of the eye and using your clay tools, gently push the remaining length into place, using the horseshoe-shaped tip to tuck up the clay under the wool eyelid. Cut off any excess length, then do the same to apply the other eyelid. When you are happy with the shaping, allow to dry.

Step 12
26

With the clay eyelids now dry, using a reverse felting needle, gently pull out the wool from around the clay eyes, to give the appearance of fur growing on the edges of the eyelids and to help the wool snugly surround the eyelids. Trim away any excess wool. Gently add more wool if needed and reverse felt the edges again.

Step 13
27, 28

Now it is time to attach the neck to the body. Fit the head onto the neck wire and assess the length of neck. Adjust as needed

26

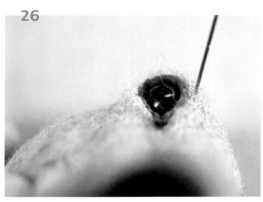

by trimming any excess neck, or adding a little more, or adjusting the wire length. Attach a couple of short lengths of Biscuit to the aperture of the head (as shown) then place head onto the neck wire and felt into place. Add more wool to shape the neck and jaw bones. You can use this opportunity to smooth over the body shape with a quilting iron or pyrography tool to get rid of any needle marks and to assess if any more

27

28

shaping is needed. This will make a huge difference to muscle definition.

Step 14
29, 30

To make the ears, felt a couple of long ear shapes on a felting brush, using a multi-sprung tool. The ears should be 4.5cm (1.77in) long and 3.5cm (1.3in) wide at the widest part at the bottom. Leave the base unfelted on each ear, to aid attachment to the head. Iron the ears, or flatten them with hair

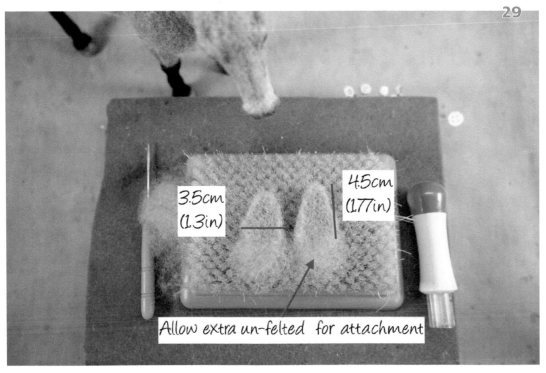

3.5cm (1.3in)

4.5cm (1.77in)

Allow extra un-felted for attachment

straighteners and check that they are not see-through. Thicken them up with more felting if needed and flatten again. Trim the ears to an ear shape. If you hold them both flat together when trimming, you will have two ears exactly the same shape and size.

Step 15
31, 32

Colour the inside of each ear with Raw Umber Ex Dark 780.1, then felt some lengths of white core around the edges of each ear, as shown, to give the appearance of lighter fur growing around the inside edges of the ears. Attach the white core in very thin amounts, and by felting them into the ear and not right through it. This can be achieved by felting with your needle flat to the ear, so that the attachment goes inside the thickness of the ear. Trim when done. Give the outer edges of each ear a colouring of Raw Umber Ex Dark.

31

32

33

Step 16
33, 34

Attach the ears to the back of the head, in whatever pose you like. I've made mine a relaxed pose. Roll together the bottom part of each ear as you attach them, until they almost meet. Place them on the head and felt around the base of each ear, holding in position as you do. You might find some long hat pins useful in this step, to hold them in place before felting. Use the unfelted base of each ear to attach to the head.

34

35

Step 17
35, 36, 37, 38

To create the upright mane, you will need to cut a shallow channel along the top of the neck, from between the ears to the top of the shoulders. Next cut a couple of lengths of Merino Raven roughly 3.5cm (1.3in) in length, card them lightly so they are ready to use and gently take a small pinch of Merino Raven, place across the cut channel and felt in the length down the centre, so that it is pushed into the channel and each side stands up and meets as you felt. Continue down the length of the channel. Next, prepare a small amount of Sand of shorter length, around 2cm (0.78in) card; take a pinch of wool and add along both sides of the mane, to give a brown tinge to the outer edges of the dark mane. When done, trim mane to length.

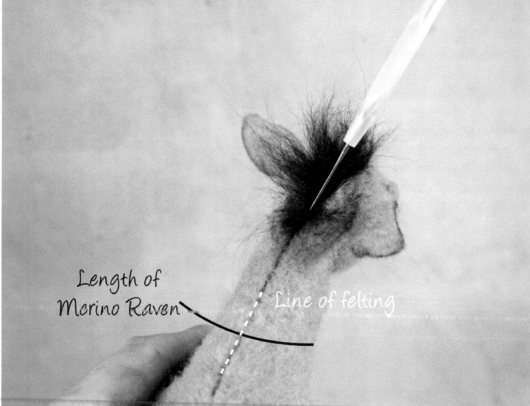

36

Length of Merino Raven

Line of felting

37

38

Step 18
39, 40, 41, 42

To finish the tail, you will need to cover with Raven core to a decent thickness to allow some long fur attachment, then attach some long lengths (same as you used for the mane) of Merino Raven to cover the tail. Use the end attachment method making sure you don't

39

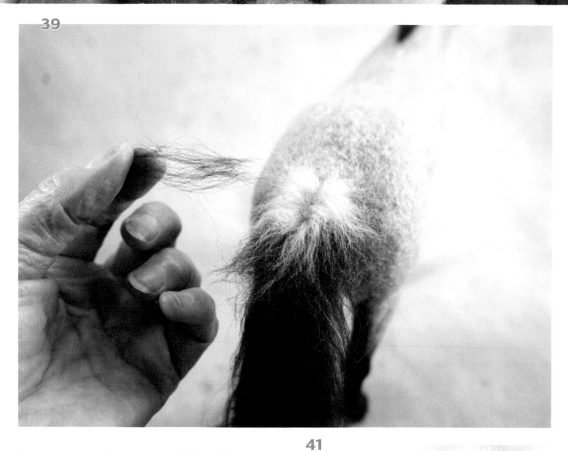

leave any gaps. The very top of the tail has a short length of lighter colouring with a line of black down the centre. Use Merino Sand for the lighter tail colouring. Trim the tail to make it look a little wild and straggly.

41

40

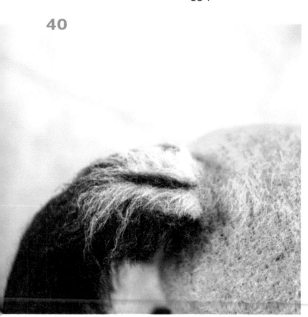

Step 19
43, 44

Add some short lengths of Merino Raven to the underside of each fetlock joint, to create the feathered feet. Trim to shape and length. Use some Mod Podge Gloss mix one part Mod Podge to five parts water, and spray the mane and tail to hold in place. Use a three-in-a-row needle tool to arrange the tail and mane before it dries. Allow to dry.

45

Step 19
45, 46, 47, 48

Using your felting brush and multi-sprung tool, and the remainder of Carded Shetland Natural Grey (any earthy colour would do), felt a flat base that will easily place all four feet of the horse. You might find the multi-unsprung tool useful for this part. Felt until firm on both sides to a thickness of no less than 1cm (0.39in). I have added a layer of Caramel to

46

this base to give a sand colouring ready for the dried grass. Add some lengths of Merino Sand to make some tufts of dry grass, using the end attachment, making sure that the foot placement is avoided. Give the grass a spray of the Mod Podge mix and pinch the wool grass ends together to make long straggly grass lengths. Allow to dry.

Step 20
49, 50, 51, 52

Finally, sew each hoof onto the base, using some black thread so that it doesn't show on the feet. Sew from the underside of the base, up through the hoof and out through the very bottom of the leg, where it meets the hoof and back down again. That way, you

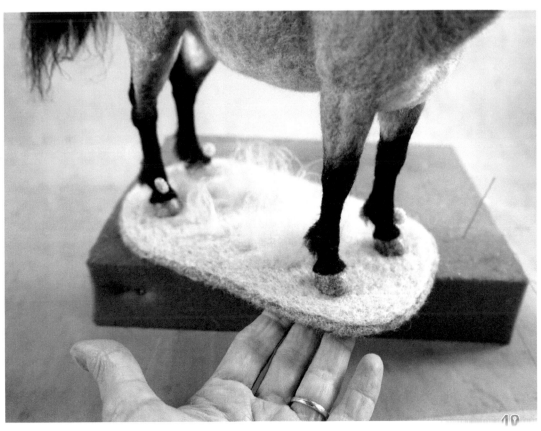

won't damage the actual hoof. Sew a couple of stitches through the leg, hoof and base and tie off tightly under the base. Repeat for the other three legs, and you're done!

TIP: Use your long pins to secure the other three legs in place on the felting sponge, whilst the other leg is hanging over the edge of the sponge (see photo). This way you can ensure the legs stay in position, and you have easier access to the one you are working on.

50

51

52

THE PAINTED DOG

THE PAINTED DOG (*Lycaon pictus*)
Also known as Cape Hunting Dog and African Wild Dog
The largest wild canine in Africa, native to sub-Saharan Africa, and absent only in the driest deserts and lowland forests. They inhabit mostly savannah and arid zones, which is likely linked to their prey and the way they hunt. They live in a strong social pack and are specialised hunters of medium-sized antelopes. They approach their prey silently, then pursue over long distances to tire the prey until it gives up. Dispatch is swift. Their main enemies are lions and hyenas. Painted Dog numbers are severely threatened by habitat fragmentation and disease. It is estimated that only around 6600 exist, and the species has been on the IUCN Red List since 1990.

1

1
The only dog in this book, this model features a short reverse felted coat, clay nails, acrylic bead eyes, grass base, and realistic pads.
The finished Painted Dog weighs 105g (3.7oz).

ITEMS NEEDED
Core wool
- Core (natural) white wool 60g (2.1oz) World of Wool Carded Jacob Batt or Norwegian Sliver
- Core wool Tan 40g (1.58oz) The Felt Box. No: 73
- Core wool Raven 15g (0.52oz) World of Wool
- Core wool any earthy colour for the base 40g (1.58oz)

Merino wool
- Merino Raven 20g (0.7oz) World of Wool
- Merino Sand 25g (0.8oz) Wingham Wool
- Merino Pearl 25g (0.8oz) World of Wool

Other items

- Wire 1.3mm (16 gauge) preferably plastic coated 44cm (17.3in) x 1, 43cm (16.9in) x 2
- Acrylic beads white or off-white 8mm (0.31in) x 2, a pair of glass beads 8mm 'spacer beads'

TOOLS

- A comprehensive range of felting needles, including three-in-a-row, multi-sprung, multi unsprung
- Tape measure
- Pliers and wire cutters (pointed end type)
- Awl
- Nail file
- Felting sponge
- Felting brush
- Scissors (small pointed)
- Long hat pins x 6 and a couple of sewing round headed pins
- Brushes, any small 'nail art' brushes
- Small pair of wire-toothed carders
- Alcohol pens, Spectrum Noir Black, GB8, BG9

- Circle template which includes 6mm (0.23in) circle
- Mod Podge Gloss/Matt and small spray bottle
- Diamond glaze
- Hair straighteners/iron
- Wax Master iron/Pyrography iron with flat pointed end
- Pan Pastels, Raw Umber 780.5, Orange Ex Dark 280.1, Neutral Grey Tint 820.7
- Sewing needle and light thread (cream or fawn)

METHOD
Step 1
2, 3

Using your three lengths of wire, 44cm x 1 and 43cm x 2, create your armature, using the longest length for the tail, back, neck and head. Fold the other two lengths in half and create a front and back pair of legs. Fold the legs to the measurements shown on the armature plan. Then trim the feet to length and arrange your armature so that it can stand squarely and

2

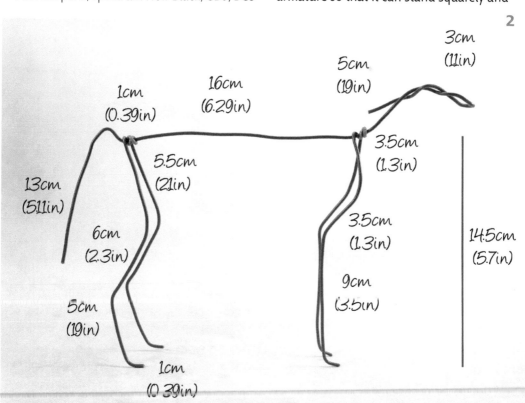

3cm
(11in)

5cm
(19in)

1cm
(0.39in)

16cm
(6.29in)

3.5cm
(1.3in)

13cm
(5.11in)

5.5cm
(21in)

6cm
(2.3in)

3.5cm
(1.3in)

14.5cm
(5.7in)

5cm
(19in)

9cm
(3.5in)

1cm
(0.39in)

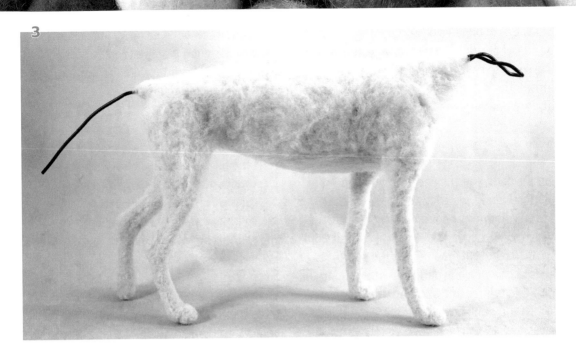

3

unaided. Cover the armature with white core wool, making some shaping for the body and legs. I have made this Painted Dog in a walking pose with head down, but you can make yours in any pose you like. Create some basic shaped feet as shown. Once you have decided on the pose, pay attention not to distort the pose as you work on your sculpture.

Step 2
4

When you are happy with your basic shaping, start adding some brown colouring using Tan. Each Painted Dog has differently placed markings, they can be mostly brown with some black and white patches, or very dark colouring, so there is no fixed pattern to follow.

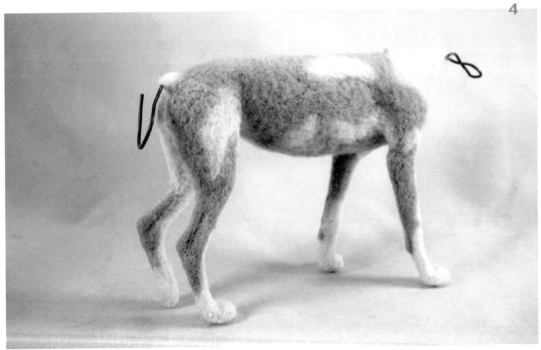

4

Study lots of pictures of Painted Dogs and decide what colours and pattern you would like yours to have. I've made this one mostly brown. The patterns are completely random and are not the same both sides.

Step 3
5, 6

For the pads, you will need a small amount of Merino Blend 1, which is a sort of dark grey/brown colouring and is a blend of one part Raven to ¼ part Sand to ¼ part Pearl, all from 1.5cm (0.59in) cut lengths. Felt the pads onto all four paws, paying particular attention to the paw that is lifted and showing the underside. Whilst you don't have to felt the other three paws, as they will be hidden by foliage, they

will show if someone wants to look closely enough (it's good practice too!). Note, the back feet are slightly shorter than the front feet, as they are in most canines.

> TIP: Merino Tops come in standard thicknesses. If you cut a length of Merino (roughly 2cm (0.78in) in length) before conditioning and call that one part, you can easily work out half a part by simply splitting a part in half, and a quarter by splitting half of the half.

Step 4
7, 8

Once you have added some pads on the feet, adjust the edging of the foot shape as needed, making sure the feet match up with the edges of the pads. When felting the pads you can easily create a nice symmetrical shaping, which doesn't always match with the foot shaping. I usually have to add a little to the edges of the toes. After you have done that, make three cuts to each paw: one down the centre and two either side, using the pads as guides. Don't cut fully between the pads underneath the paw, but make a deep cut above, so that the toes are separated. Felt the cut edges to round off the toes and to give them some shaping. Don't forget the little pads at the back of each front leg.

5

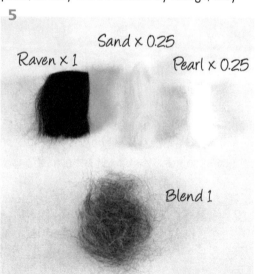

Raven x 1

Sand x 0.25

Pearl x 0.25

Blend 1

6

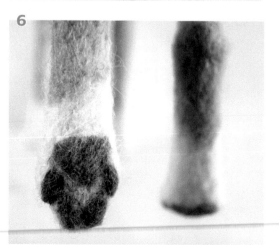

7

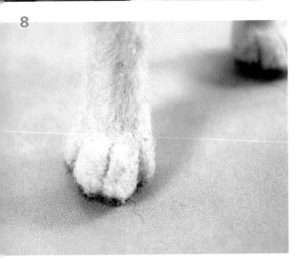

8

mind as you work and experience shrinkage. Add the Raven to cover the bottom part of the muzzle, as far as the cheeks, but not the complete top part. We will be adding more detailed colouring later. With the head shape built up, cut two horizontal slits for each eye and place a spacer bead into each cut. Once happy with the shaping of the head and eye sockets, remove the spacer beads and, using a black alcohol pen, colour the inside of each socket. Cut a channel into the base of the head, so that it can be placed onto the head wire. Assess for head placement and neck length and adjust the neck wire as needed.

TIP: As a general rule of thumb, the eyes of most canines sit centre to the length of head. So exactly half way between the back of the head and the nose.

Step 5
9, 10, 11, 12

You should now have a fairly good shaped Painted Dog, with feet and pads and the two main colours applied.

For the head, create a basic head shape using some Core Tan and add some Core Raven to colour and shape the muzzle. The finished head will need to be roughly 6cm (2.36in) long from back of head to tip of nose. Keep this in

Step 6
13, 14

Using a felting brush, multi-sprung tool and an awl, create a pair of ears using

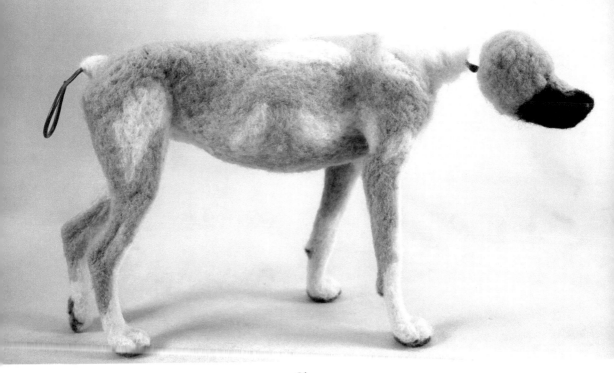

9

10

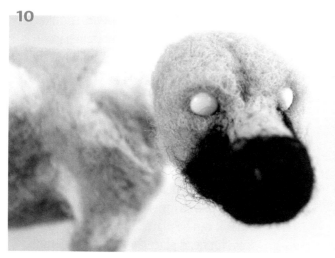

11

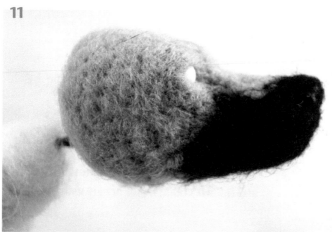

some Merino Raven to the measurements shown. Felt them thick enough not to be see-through when held up to a light. Leave the bottom part of each ear unfelted, as this will aid attachment to the head. A Painted Dog's ears are enormous for the size of its head, note also that they taper in slightly at the bottom. With the basic ears done, flatten them using an iron or some hair straighteners, and adjust any thin parts by felting some more thickness. Flatten again. With both ears facing you, add a line of Merino Sand along both outer edges of each ear, then alongside the line of Merino Sand on the inside, add a line of Merino Raven. Attach this merino in the same way as described in Step 15 of the Przewalski's Horse chapter (page 48).

12

13

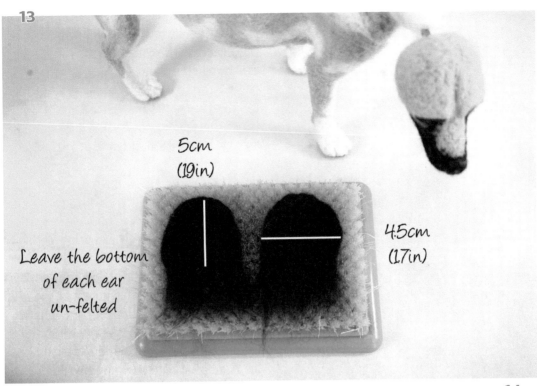

5cm
(19in)

4.5cm
(1.7in)

Leave the bottom
of each ear
un-felted

14

Line of Merino Sand

Fine line of Merino Raven

Step 7

15

Trim the excess fur inside the ears and attach to the head, making the inner ear lengths longer than the outer lengths. You might find some long hat pins useful for placing the ears equally and the same length. You also might need to add a little bulk to the back part of

15

the head to help the ears sit correctly. Felt into place and gently brush the ear fur on the inner side of each ear, to cover over the ear opening, as shown in the photo.

> TIP: If you notice any Merino Sand showing through the back of the ears, colour it with a black felt tipped pen, or alcohol pen.

Step 8
16

Add long fur around the head using Merino Sand, up to the eyes and over the cheeks as far as the black muzzle marking. You can use the 'down the middle' attachment for around the head and end attachment for the more detailed areas such as around the eyes and cheeks. Attach a line of Merino Raven down the middle of the head. Trim when done. The photo below shows one side trimmed and one side untrimmed. Felt some detail to the nose with Merino Raven and place a couple of round headed sewing pins for the nostrils. Cut

16

Not trimmed

Trimmed

two slits either side of the nose and felt into shape.

Step 9
17, 18, 19, 20

Once you have felted a very firm nose with a good shape, give the surface a trim and give a covering of Mod Podge Matt. Once fully dried, file the nose using a nail file, to smooth away the roughness. Repeat the Mod Podge and filing steps again if you need to add a little more detailing. When done, colour the nose using a black alcohol pen. Attach the head to the body using some Core Tan.

18

17

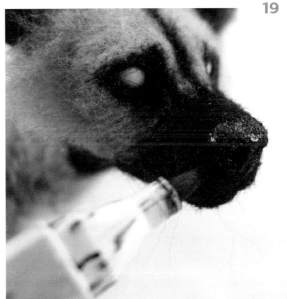

19

20

21

Step 10
21, 22, 23

Continue using the black alcohol pen to add some black markings to the body. Again, where you add the black markings is up to you, so be sure to study lots of photos of Painted Dogs to find some markings that you'd like to copy. When you have completed your black markings, reverse felt the complete coat. This will do two things, create some short body fur and will soften the harsh black markings. Do the reverse felting gently and deliberately and in the direction of fur growth, so in general, pulling out the reverse needle towards the back end of the sculpture.

22

23

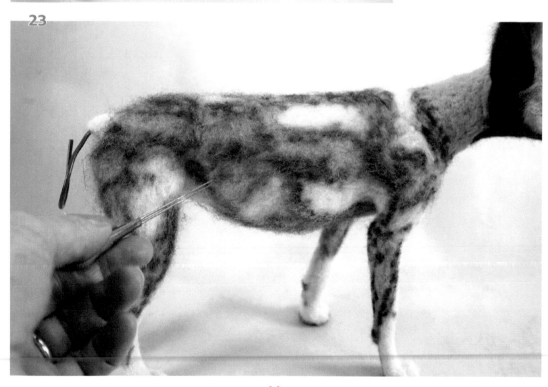

Step 11
24, 25

Using a mini Wax Master/Pyrography iron, smooth over the body to straighten the reverse felted wool, to create a fur-like appearance. You will need a small flat, pointed end, so that the wool can be straightened. Give the sculpture a trim when done. Very lightly reverse felt down the legs and straighten the reverse felted wool, and also use the mini iron to add some detailed shaping to the legs and feet. Trim the created fur to length.

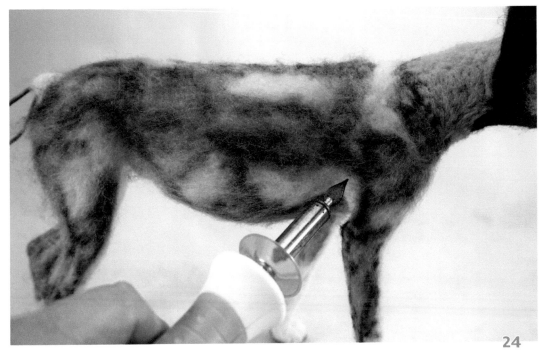

24

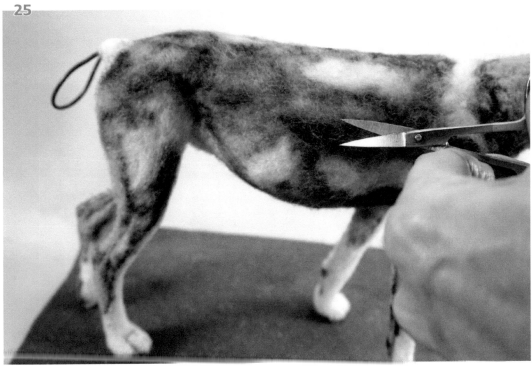

25

Step 12
26, 27

You will now need to add some longer fur to the neck. For this you will need some 2.5cm (0.98in) lengths of prepared carded Sand, Raven, Blend 1 (see STEP 3 for the amounts of colours needed for Blend 1) and an even mix of Blend 1 and Sand. The sand is to be attached to the top of the neck, the Raven to the underside and Blend 1 to be placed on the side of the neck along the Raven, with the mix of Blend 1 and Sand between the Sand and

26

Sand

Mix of Blend 1 & Sand

Blend 1

Raven

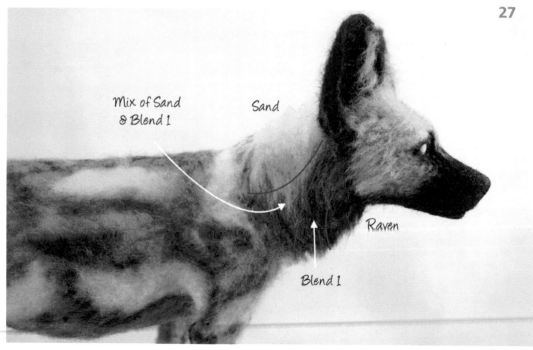

27

Mix of Sand & Blend 1

Sand

Raven

Blend 1

Blend 1. This will achieve a nice gradation of colouring from light to dark on the sides of the neck. The annotated photo shows where the blends are placed. Trim to length when finished.

Step 13
28, 29, 30

To create the eyes, using your acrylic beads, circle template, awl and alcohol pens GB6 and BG9, place one of the beads onto the end of your awl. Place the 6mm (0.23in) circle template firmly over the bead and colour the inside of the circle with the GB6. Make sure

you have given a good colouring first time by circling the tip of the pen inside the circle. Remove the template and allow to dry. Give a covering of Diamond Glaze and allow to dry. With the BG9 alcohol pen, make a pupil by dotting the colour in the centre of each brown circle. Cover again with Diamond Glaze. Finish off with the final colouring of GB6 to intensify the brown a little, and then with some BG9 around the edge of the pupil to give a muddy/watery effect. Give a final coat of Diamond Glaze and dry. Fit eyes into place using a little dab of craft glue to the inside of each socket. Allow to dry completely.

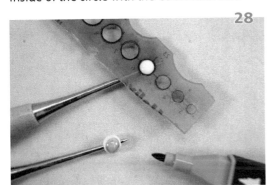

28

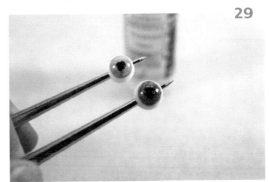

29

30

TIP: Don't go back and try to fill in faults with your alcohol pen once applied (before applying Diamond Glaze), as this will cause the applied colours to be wiped off. If you have made a mistake, give the colouring you have done a covering of Diamond Glaze, allow to dry and colour again over the mistakes or wherever needed.

Step 14
31

Using an earthy coloured core wool, a felting brush and multi-sprung tool and a multi-unsprung tool, create a base on which the sculpture can stand. Tightly felt both sides of the base and tidy around the edges. You can make it any shape you like.

31

Step 15
32, 33

To finish the tail, give an initial covering of Core Tan, and at the end of the tail, loop through a length of Pearl Tops and use the end of the wire to nip back in place. This will provide a tip to the furred tail. Add some more bulk to the tail in both Core Raven and Tan. Usually the top third of the tail is tan fur,

32

Place a length of Pearl through the bend at the end of the tail

33

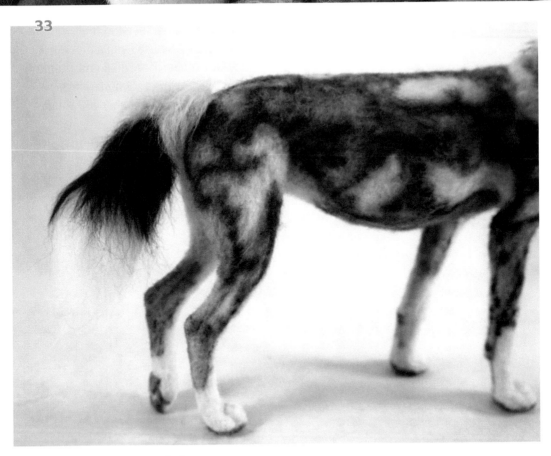

34

the middle is black and the tip white. Attach long fur (3.5cm (1.37in) lengths of prepared carded Merino wool of Raven, Sand and Pearl) keeping to the pattern you have made. Trim when done.

Step 16

34

Check the pads are neatly felted, and trim the surfaces. Give the pads of the raised foot a coat of Mod Podge Matt. Leave to dry, then give them a light filing with a nail file. You don't have to do this to all the pads, just the one on the back paw which is showing. The other three pads will be sewn to the base, so won't be seen.

Step 17
35, 36

Using some Pan Pastels and alcohol pens, add some more marking and details to the legs. Painted Dogs often have brown and black spots on their feet and their legs are often very grey. So use Pan Pastels Black 800.5, Raw Umber Tint 780.8 and Titanium White 100.5. For the brown markings use a combination of Raw Umber 780.5 and

35

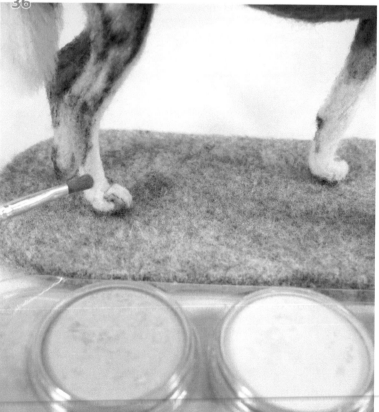

36

alcohol pen GB8. When finished, give the white on the lower part of the legs a light dusting of Raw Umber Tint 780.8 to tone down the bright white as they live in very dusty environments.

Step 18
37, 38

To make some dried grass on the base, felt in lengths of Sand Tops, long enough to make grass that is at least 3cm (1.18in) in length, but add varying lengths to make it look natural. Use the end attachment method and attach the grass in small clumps, leaving enough space for the feet to be placed on the base. Mix one part Mod Podge Gloss to five parts water into a small fine spray bottle and give the grass a spray with the mixture. Pinch the ends of the grass with your fingers, to help the ends come together. Allow to dry. You can also give the tail a little spray to keep the fur in place.

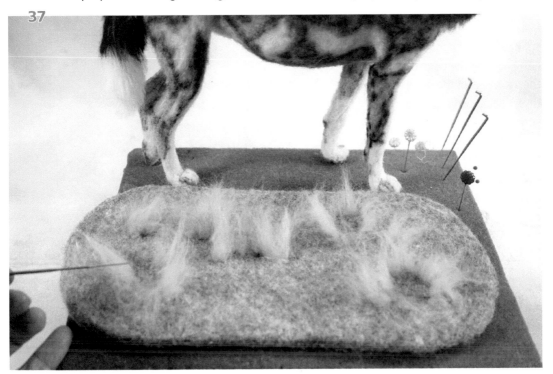

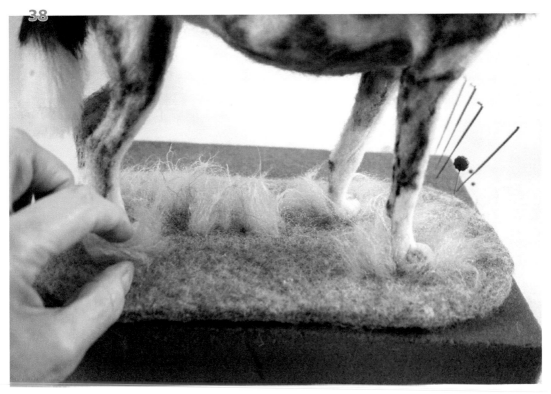

Step 19

39, 40, 41, 42, 43

Place your Painted Dog exactly where he needs to be on the felted base. Place the base on a felting sponge, with one foot hanging over the edge of the sponge and the other three feet secured on the sponge with long pins. This will allow you easy access to a foot, as you sew it to the base.

With needle and thread, starting up through the bottom of the base, sew up through one side of a foot, across the foot and back down through the other side of the foot and the base. You are aiming to track over the ends of each foot wire, so that the foot will be securely sewn in place. Repeat to double stitch each foot, then tie off both ends of the thread under the base. Repeat for the other three feet. Trim excess thread ... and you're done!

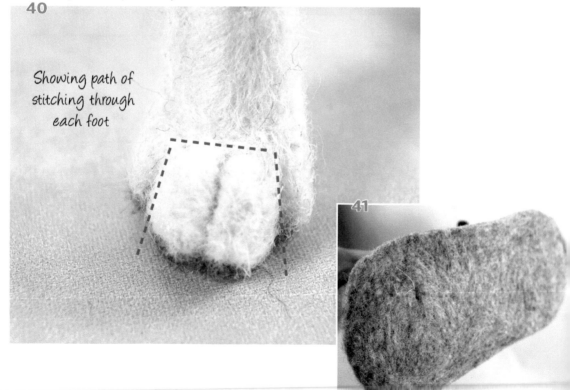

Showing path of stitching through each foot

42

43

THE SECRETARY BIRD

THE SECRETARY BIRD (*Sagittarius serpentarius*)
A large, mostly terrestrial bird that inhabits open grassland and savannah of sub-Saharan Africa. It is an instantly recognisable bird with long crane-like legs that give it a height of 1.3m (4ft 3in), with grey and black plumage, a red-orange face and beautiful long eyelashes. Its prey consists of any small mammals, frogs, lizards and occasionally the young of larger mammals, such as cheetahs. Secretary birds are also adept at catching snakes of all types, but they do not eat carrion. They were classed as endangered in 2020 due to bush encroachment and loss of the open habitat that they prefer. Also causing a decline in numbers is fragmentation of habitat due to roads, and an increase in over-grazing of grasslands. Estimates of numbers for all 38 inhabited African countries suggests that total population size does not exceed a five figure number and is in decline.

The completed Secretary Bird weighs 182g (6.41oz).
1

1

ITEMS NEEDED
Core wool
- Slivers Mink 30g (1oz) (World of Wool)
- Slivers Raven 50g (1.7oz) (World of Wool)
- Slivers White 100g (3.5oz) (World of Wool)
- Slivers Begonia 5g (0.17oz) (World of Wool)
- Slivers Marigold 15g (0.5oz) (World of Wool)
- Slivers Buttercup 5g 0.17oz) (World of Wool)
- Core Caramel (or a fawn) 60g (2.1oz) (The Felt Box No: 22)
- Core Rabbit 80g (2.8oz) (World of Wool)

Merino wool
- Merino Ash 60g (2.1oz) (World of Wool)
- Merino Pearl 20g (0.7oz) (World of Wool)
- Merino Raven 50g (1.7oz) (World of Wool)

Other items

- Wire: 1.5mm (15 gauge) – legs 64cm (25in) x1; body 45cm (17.7in) x 1; anchor for wings 18cm (7in) x 1; wing spread 50cm (19.6in) x 1; snake 48cm (18.8in) x 1
- Wire 1.2mm (18 gauge) – toes 9cm (3.5in) x 2, 8cm (3.1in) x 2
- Pack of floristry/cake paper-coated wire, 24 or 26 gauge
- Cabochons (low domed) 10mm and 8mm
- 4 x 6cm (1.5in x 2.3in) gloss photo paper (and printer) to print eyes (see Method)
- A4 paper to print feather templates
- A4 sheets of pre-felt, black x 2, mid-grey x 2
- A roll of iron-on hemming tape (any colour)

TOOLS

- A comprehensive range of felting needles, including three-in-a-row, multi-sprung, multi unsprung
- Tape measure
- Pliers and wire cutters (pointed end type)
- Awl
- Bulldog clip
- Nail file
- Felting sponge
- Felting brush
- Scissors (small pointed)
- Long hat pins x 6 and couple of sewing round-headed pins
- Brushes, any small 'nail art' brushes
- Small pair of wire-toothed carders
- Alcohol pens, Spectrum Noir Black, GB8, BG9 and Black
- Mod Podge Satin and small spray bottle
- Diamond glaze
- Craft glue
- Steam iron and heat proof material to iron on
- Pastel, white
- Sewing needle and thread (cream or fawn)

METHOD

Please read this chapter fully before starting.
First, download the 'Secretary Bird Feather

Plan' and the 'Bird & Snake Eye' PDFs from www.chicktincreations.com/Downloads for 3rd Book, and enter the code SBFF. Print pages 2 to 5 to avoid printing the PDF cover page. For this you will need four sheets of A4 paper. The Secretary Bird/Snake Eyes should be printed on glossy 6 x 4in photographic paper. These eyes will not print in the right size unless 6 x 4in paper is used. Set aside until needed. Cut all your lengths of wire ready to use.

Step 1
2, 3, 4

Take the longest length of wire 64cm (25in) and fold in half to form the legs. Working from the bottom upwards, bend both legs together to the measurements shown. To make the toes, each foot has one 9cm (3.5in) and one 8cm (3.1in) wire. Take the 9cm (3.5in), fold in half and wrap half around the foot length of the leg and push the remaining half to the back. This

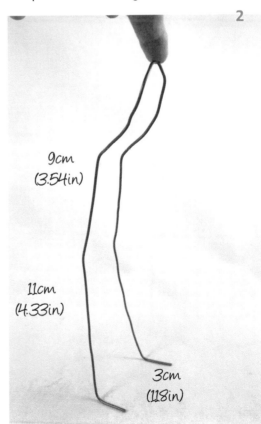

3

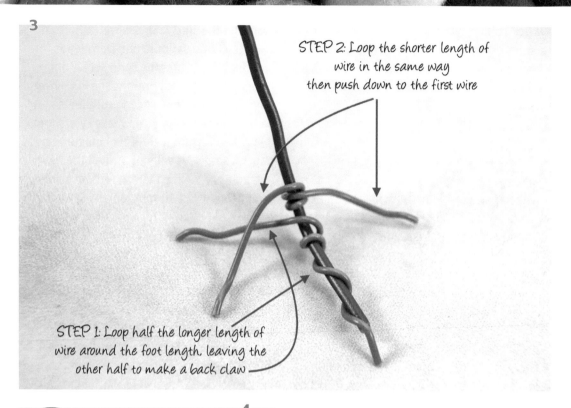

STEP 2: Loop the shorter length of wire in the same way then push down to the first wire

STEP 1: Loop half the longer length of wire around the foot length, leaving the other half to make a back claw

4

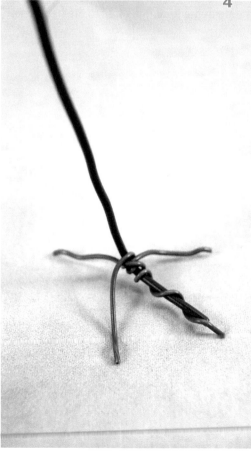

will make the middle longest toe and the back toe. Now take the other 8cm (3.1in) wire, fold in half and wrap around the the leg, then slide down to above the previous wire. These will be the two outer toes. Trim the toes to length and nip the joins tight with your pliers.

Step 2

5

Using the 45cm (17.7in) length of wire, measure 25cm (9.84in) from one end (the tail end) and wrap the legs twice tightly at this point, making sure the legs are equal in length. Nip the join tight with some pliers if needed. The neck should measure no less than 15cm (5.9in) from the join to the beginning of the head. Fold the remaining length in half to make the head. Fold the 18cm (7in) length of wire in half and wrap to the body just behind the legs, nipping tightly to secure in place. This will provide a base on which to attach the wings. (Note: mine slid down as I took the photo! An arrow and dot is showing where the wing base should be positioned, just behind the legs.)

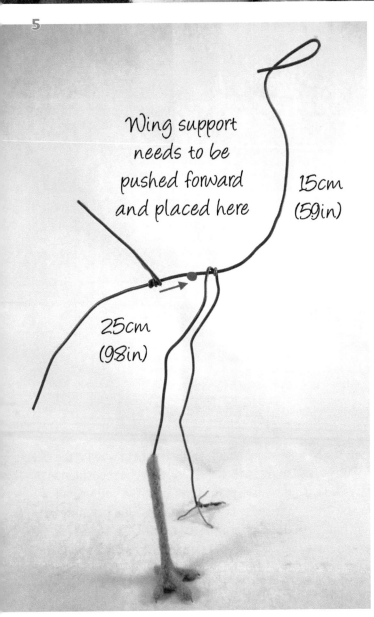

5

Wing support
needs to be
pushed forward
and placed here

15cm
(5.9in)

25cm
(9.8in)

Step 3
6, 7

Cover the bottom half of the legs to just above the hock joint, very thinly, with some Mink. Make sure you keep this covering as thin as possible, adding some shaping to the toes and a little webbing between them. Leave the ends of the wire, around 5mm (0.19in), poking out from end of each toe. These will be the toe nails. Curve them downwards slightly and colour them with a black marker pen.

Step 4
8, 9

Start adding some White to shape the body, neck and the tail. Build the shaping up to a fairly firm touch. The finished base tail should measure roughly 9cm (3.5in) long and 3cm (0.78in) wide to support the tail feathers. You will need to trim the tail wire for this. Add some Raven to shape the top half of the legs. Curl each end of the wing bases around, to prevent them catching as you work, but make sure you don't lose them in the body. Secretary

6

7

8

9

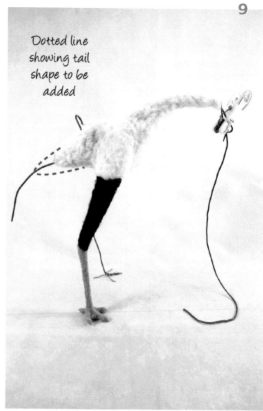

Dotted line
showing tail
shape to be
added

Birds are very leggy, with slender bodies. Study lots of photos to assess their shaping. It was at this point I realised that the Secretary Bird wasn't going to be able to stand alone, so I decided to create a snake which it could hold in its beak. This created a tripod effect and the much needed support for the bird and snake

to stand unaided. The length of wire for the snake is 48cm (18.8in), though I repositioned the snake in the beak later. The bottom half of the snake is used to stabilise the sculpture by curling it around flat to the base. So instead of just two legs to support the bird, we will have two legs and a snake!

10

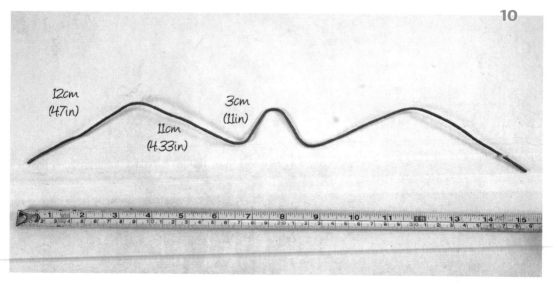

12cm
(4.7in)

11cm
(4.33in)

3cm
(1.1in)

Step 5
10

To create the spread wings, you will need a single length of wire that attaches to the body (via the wing supports) and which will provide attachment for both wings. For this, use the 50cm (19.6in) length of thicker wire, fold in half and bend to the measurements shown, then open up to make flat. Cover these wing wires with White core, felting into a flat shape of around 2cm (0.78in) wide, which will allow attachment of feathers. Leave the centre part much thinner as this will be attached to the body using the wing bases and will not need to support any feathers.

Step 6
11, 12

Using the 'Sec Bird Feather Templates', cut out the feathers, making a note of how many you need to cut. The feathers are coloured with corresponding pre-felt colour and number needed. Cut out all the feathers and be mindful of their order shown in the 'Sec Bird Wing Plan'. Set aside the tail feathers and wing top feathers. Split the remaining feathers into two wings, place each pair together, (all paired except the two smallest feathers) ready for the next stage. With your florist wires cut to lengths, pair them up with the feathers

11

you have cut: tail feather 20cm (7.8in) x 2, tail feather 15cm (5.9in) x 2, inner wing feather 16cm (6.2in) x 16, mid wing feather 19cm (7.4in) x 2, wing tip feather 19cm (7.4in) x 8.

With a heated steam iron at the ready, take a paired feather at a time, open them up and place on one side a length of florist wire to the position shown on the feather template. Then cover the wire with a couple of lengths of hemming tape, enough to cover most of the feather area, but keeping inside the feather. Trim as needed. Then gently place the other half of the feather on top of the hemming tape and wire, and iron allowing the steam to bond the two feathers together. Repeat with all the other feathers, so that you should be left with two long grey tail feathers, two shorter grey tail feathers, 16 black inner wing feathers, two

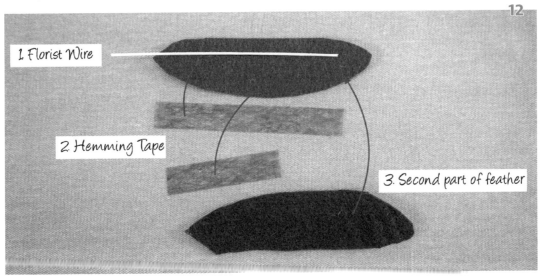

1. Florist Wire
2. Hemming Tape
3. Second part of feather

12

13

black mid wing feathers, and eight wing tip feathers. Trim feathers to tidy up if needed.

Step 7
13, 14, 15, 16

Arrange the feathers as shown, so that you know where they will be placed, referring to the Wing Plan. Using the ends of the wires on the feathers, thread them through the felted wool on the topside of the wings, as shown. When you are happy with the placement of the feathers, curl each end of the wires over, so that they hold each feather in place within the wool. Turn the wing over and cover the

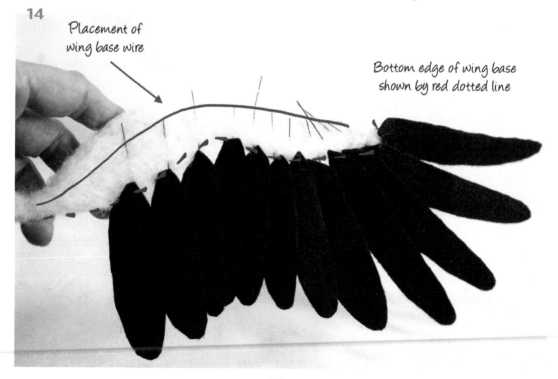

14

Placement of wing base wire

Bottom edge of wing base shown by red dotted line

15

Underside of the wing

16

Top side of the wing

underside of the wing, covering the top ends of the feathers in Merino Ash. You will need to prepare the wool before you can felt it, by cutting 2cm (0.78in) lengths of Merino, then carding those lengths to make them easier to felt (see preparing wool chapter).

Step 8
17, 18

To attach the row of small grey feathers to the topside of the wings, you will need to prepare them first. Felt a little Merino Ash onto the surface of each feather so that it hangs over

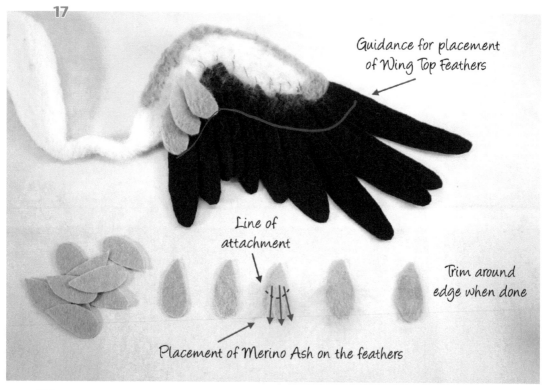

17

Guidance for placement of Wing Top Feathers

Line of attachment

Trim around edge when done

Placement of Merino Ash on the feathers

18

tips. When you are happy with their placement, you can put some hemming tape underneath them and iron into place.

Step 9
19, 20, 21

Using a felting brush, awl and sprung multi-needle, felt a flat 'boomerang' shape that will fit exactly over the leading

the bottom edges of each wing. This is to soften the harsh cut edges of the pre-felt and make them look more feather-like. Trim around the bottom edge when done. Place them along the wing so that they cover the tops of the longer black wing feathers. Photo 17 shows the guidance line for the placement of the feather

edge of the wing and half cover the row of small grey feathers you have just attached. Try to leave the bottom edge of the shape a little unfelted, so that when placed onto the wing, it will easily blend with the feathers. Felt onto the wing so that you are unable to see any joins. Repeat for the other side.

19

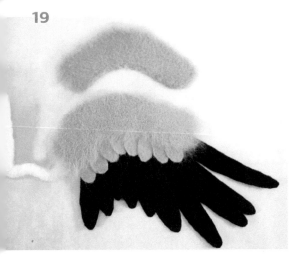

20

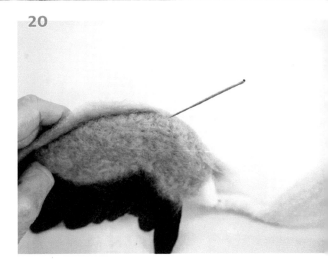

21

Step 10
22, 23, 24

With a good core tail shape ready to support the tail feathers, create these feathers by ironing them together as you did previously in STEP 6, along with the two black inner wing feathers. Using some Pan Pastel black and white, colour the pattern onto the tail feathers as shown. Arrange onto the tail, so that the long feathers make a total tail length of around 20cm (7.8in) taken from the base of the tail, where the body starts. Thread the ends of the

22

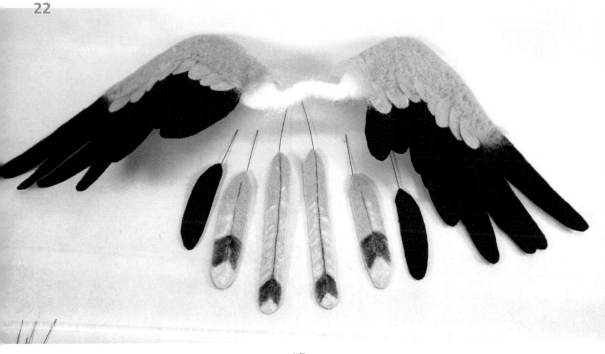

23

Red dotted line
shows the core
tail shape under
the feathers

24

Dotted line shows
placement of stitches
to hold tail feathers
in place

feather wires through the tail base, and bend over so that the feathers are held secure as shown. With needle and thread, stitch the tops

and inner edges of the tail feathers into place on the tail base.

25

Step 11
25

Now start to add some feathering to the body, using Merino Ash and the end attachment method. Cover the underside and top of the tail and start to cover the body, from above the top of the legs upwards. Stop at the wing support wires, ready to attach the wings.

26

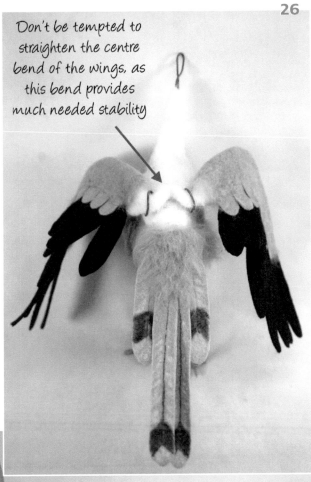

Don't be tempted to straighten the centre bend of the wings, as this bend provides much needed stability

Step 12

26, 27, 28, 29

Attach the wings to the body, using the wing support wire loops to hold them in place, as shown. When happy with their placement, tighten the wing base loops, then cover with some more core wool. Also cover and add some bulk and shaping where the wings meet the body on the underside to ensure the wings are completely attached. Continue covering the body with Merino Ash.

27

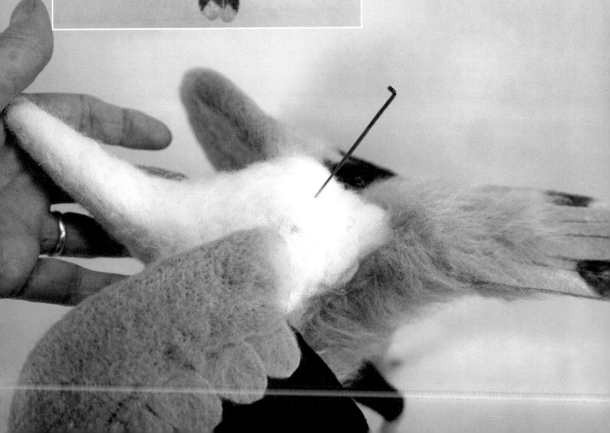

28

29

Step 13
30, 31, 32

On top of the body, where the wings are bridged, cover with Merino Ash. Above that add a line of Core Raven as shown, to fit between the two wings. Arrange the five rump feathers in a line so that they will fit within the wing bridge, but leaving enough room for an inner wing feather on each side, to close the gap. Add a line of Core Raven along the top of the rump feathers to secure them together. Place the row of rump feathers between the wings, and felt into place.

30

31

32

Step 14
33, 34

With the rump feathers felted in place, attach an inner wing each side of the rump feathers, using the wire of the feather and a little more Core Raven to secure them. Continue adding Merino Ash over the top of the feathers and up the back of the bird.

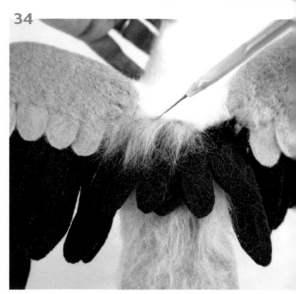

34

33

35

Step 15
35, 36, 37

To make the snake, cover the 48cm (18.8in) length of wire with some Caramel. Fold the end of the wire for the head and shape the head, making an indent for the eyes to be placed. Using a pair of snake eyes printed on the 4 x 6cm photo paper, add a dot of Diamond Glaze to each eye, and place over them an 8mm (0.3in) cabochon, gently pushing any bubbles out. Allow to dry, then cut out each eye. Place them into the indents made on the snake's head. Glue into place using any craft glue and allow to dry. Build up around the eye and add an indented line for the mouth. Cut a shallow line first, if you feel this helps with defining the mouth. You could at this point add some

90

36

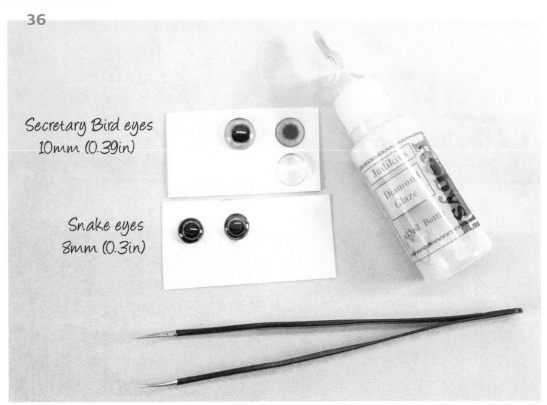

Secretary Bird eyes
10mm (0.39in)

Snake eyes
8mm (0.3in)

37

markings to your snake, by felting some on or using alcohol pens. I've left this one plain.

Step 16
38, 39, 40

To create the bird head, using some Core White, create a basic head shape, including a beak that is 6cm (2.3in) from back of head to the tip of the beak. A downward curve will be added to the beak as we add more details. As you add more detail, be aware that the head will shrink a little, so ensure you maintain the size as you work.

38

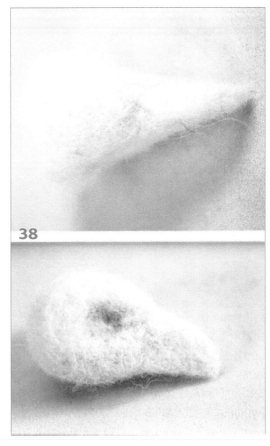

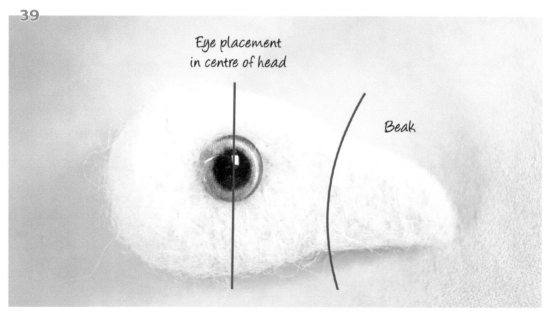

39

Eye placement
in centre of head

Beak

40

Prepare the eyes by choosing a pair from the 'S Bird/Snake Eyes' on the photo paper, add a dab of Diamond Glaze, place a couple of 10mm (0.39in) cabochons over each eye, gently pushing out any bubbles. When dry, cut out and place on the head. Discounting the beak, the eye is placed in the centre of the head

(see Photo 39), and looking slightly forwards. Ensure you have felted a depression for the eyes to be easily positioned, then glue in place. Allow to dry before doing any more work on the head.

Step 17
41, 42, 43, 44

With the eye fixed in place, start adding more detail and colour to the head. Apply a covering of Marigold to surround the eye, to make some eyelids and up to the beak. Add some wrinkles around the eyes and add some Merino Ash to add shaping to the downward-curved beak. Felt the beak as firmly and densely as you can. Cut a bottom beak and add some Marigold to make the corners of the mouth. To add some definition, add a little Begonia into the creases on the Marigold. Cut a couple of small slits to define the nostrils and felt them into shape. You can add a wisp of Raven inside the nostrils for definition. When you are happy with the beak, give it a surface trim and a coat of Mod Podge Satin. When dry, file smooth with a nail file. Apply another coat of Mod Podge Satin, taking care to add in any missed areas or dips. Dry, file and repeat if needed.

41

42

43

44

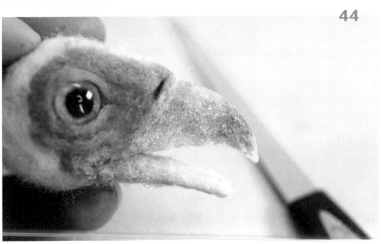

Step 18
45, 46, 47

Add a very thin line of Merino Raven to the inner eyelid of each eye, to give definition of depth. Just above the eyelid, add a line of Merino Raven to create the long eyelashes, top and bottom of each eye. Trim to length.

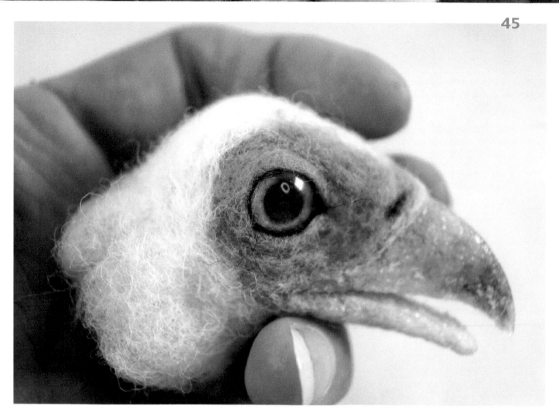

45

46

47

Step 19
48, 49, 50

Next, add some feathering to the top of the head using some Merino Ash and the end attachment method. At this stage you can attach the head to the neck.

Cut a channel through the bottom of the head to accommodate the neck wire. Place the head on the neck and cover any exposed wire with core white, making sure the neck doesn't become too long. The neck should roughly measure a couple of head lengths, including the beak.

Continue adding Merino Ash to cover the neck, with a little Merino Pearl underneath the chin area. When the neck has been completely covered, gently comb the Merino wool using a three-in-line tool, and trim to length. You

48

49

can then spray this area with a mix of one part Mod Podge Gloss, to five parts water in a small fine spray bottle. Leave to dry.

Step 20
51

Using a felting brush, awl and multi-tool, create a base with some Rabbit, large enough to accommodate the bird's feet and the coiled snake. Pin the bird to the base, holding the

50

51

snake to see how he looks. Until everything is fixed into place, you might find it all bit wobbly.

Step 21
52, 53

To create the characteristic head feathers, firstly cut out the Sec Bird Head Feathers from

52

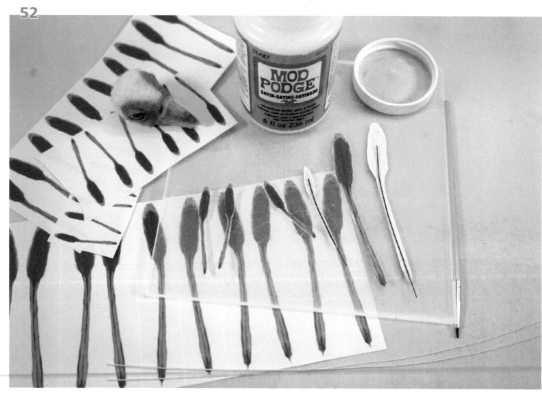

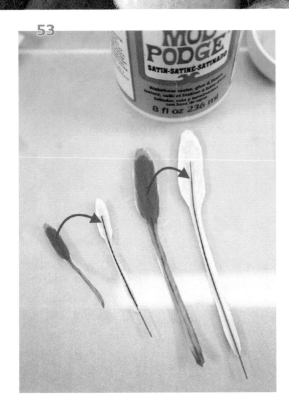

53

your printed A4 sheets. Cut within the grey borders. There are extra feathers in case of any cutting mistakes, but you'll find there are three sizes: large, medium and small. I have used five of each size (two cut outs make one feather).

With your feathers cut, you will notice that they are curved and each pair fits together to make a single feather. You will need some florist wire, a thin paint brush and some Mod Podge Satin. Cut some wire for each feather, enough so that it sits halfway into the end of the feather, all the way down the shaft and leaving around 1cm (0.39in) free wire at the end. This will be used to poke into the back of the head.

With florist wire in place, add a thin layer of glue to surround the wire and the feather, then place the other half of the feather over the glue, press gently together and leave to dry.

54

You should now have paper feathers coloured both sides, with a little excess wire to place into the back of the head.

Step 22
54, 55, 56, 57

Now you can gently part the Merino wool and poke each head feather into the back of the head, placing the larger ones towards the bottom and the smaller ones towards the top. When happy with their placement, remove each feather one-by-one, add a dab of glue to the ends of the wires, then replace and leave to dry. Using a narrow paint brush, add a little watered down Mod Podge Satin and paint the eyelashes so that they stick out and stay in place. Trim when dry. You might notice that the beak has to open too wide to accommodate the snake. To remedy that, cut a dent into the snake, to allow the beak to hold on more naturally.

55

56

57

Step 23
58, 59, 60, 61, 62

You are now ready to sew the bird and snake to the base. Using some light brown thread and needle, sew each foot into position on the base. Sew from underneath the base, up through one side of the main middle toe, across the foot and down the other side of the foot, trying to keep any thread hidden in the wool. You are aiming to loop over the toe wire to make the stitching secure. Make a couple of stitches in this way, and finally tie a couple of knots on the underside of the base.

Do the same for the other foot and the snake. Sew the snake in a couple of places

60

58

59

61

where it touches the base. You will need to support the bird and snake as you are doing this.

Finally sew the beak onto the snake. Sew from the underside, up through the bottom beak, the snake and through the head very close to the top of the beak and back down again. Make a couple of stitches for security, then tie a couple of knots on the underside of the beak. If you tie tightly enough, you will be left with a beak that appears to be gripping onto a snake ... and you're done!

62

HOW TO PREPARE &
BLEND MERINO WOOL

I have heard many felters mention how difficult it is to handle Merino tops (sometimes called roving in the US), especially for long coats. I too found it difficult at first, but I didn't give up. It can end up very flat and featureless and make a sculpture look awful, but with a little know-how, preparation and texturing, your sculptures will be transformed. The really magical quality of Merino, is its ability to blend with the huge range of dyed colours available, so your colour palette potential is huge. I haven't encountered any colour that cannot be achieved with Merino tops.

To prepare the Merino tops, you will need lengths of Merino wool and two small metal toothed carders, or small metal dog brushes work just as well. I found larger carders very difficult to manage, and the ones shown in this book are 9cm (3.54in) x 4.5cm (1.77in) with a 10cm (3.93in) handle.
1, 2

Merino tops wool comes in long lengths wound into a ball or wrapped up. It unravels into one long length. The width of these lengths is usually the same wherever it is purchased, as the process is an industrial one. For blending,

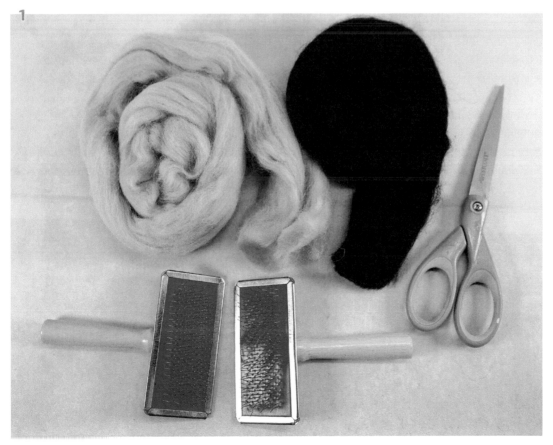

1

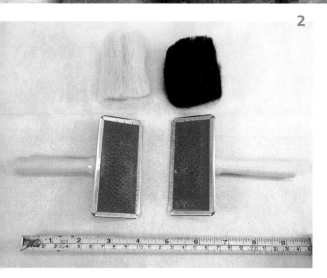

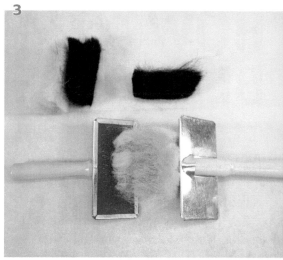

depending on the method of attachment, you will need to cut your Merino to lengths. If using the felt down the centre of the length attachment, you should cut double the finished fur length you want, plus 1cm (0.39in). If using the top of the length attachment, you need to cut the length you want plus 1cm (0.39in). The extra 1cm (0.39in) is to allow for some loss in attachment as well as allowance for trimming. So, for example, using down the middle attachment, and needing a coat length no longer than 2cm (0.78in), cut a length of 5cm (1.96in). Using end attachment for a coat no longer than 3cm (1.18in), cut 4cm (1.57in) lengths. Be aware that Merino isn't very suitable for coat lengths of over 4cm (1.57in) because the fibres are, generally, not a lot longer. You would need to use a different wool or fibre for much longer coats.

With small carders and your Merino lengths

cut, you can easily card a length at a time. To blend two colours or more, you will need to split the lengths in half, and add half one colour and half the other. Carding/blending two full lengths together with small carders will be very difficult. Here I am making a 50/50 blend of sand and black. **3**

To prepare (card) the Merino colours for blending, place one half length on one carding brush. **4**

Gently brush over it with the other brush so that you separate the fibres and they eventually get transferred. Don't be rough with this, take your time and do it gently. **5**

Brushing roughly will break the fibres into smaller lengths, and can make them tangle. Once you have brushed all the fibres loose onto the other brush, swap the brushes around and repeat the same step, or you can lift

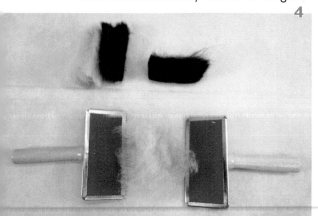

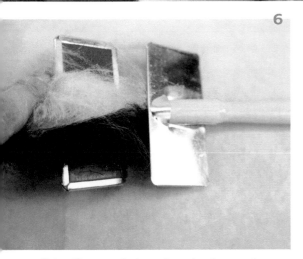

6

this time you want the two colours to blend completely. Keep a mental note of the ratio of colours used, and make sure you don't put too much onto your carders, for ease of blending. **7**

After each cycle of carding/transferring, lift off your blend and replace on the brush making sure the colours are evenly mixed. You can do this in sections to make it easier to handle, but make sure you give the whole batch a good mix. **8**

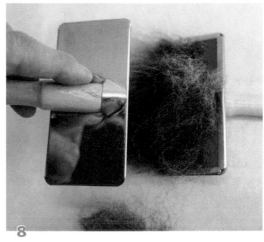

8

off the fibres and place them back onto the other brush if you prefer. The lifting off with your fingers also gives you an opportunity to rearrange the fibres for more carding and mixing of colours when blending. You might need to do this two or three times, until all the fibres are loose, fluffed, and so that you cannot see any cut edges at all. Card both colours this way. This conditioned wool is now ready to use. If you wanted to attach some single coloured wool onto your sculpture as long fur, go straight to Photo 10 for the final stage before attachment. **6**

To blend two colours, if doing a 50:50 mix, place equal amounts of both colours onto one brush by placing a bit of one colour, then a bit of the other alternately on top of each other, then card as you would a single colour, but

Keep repeating this until you have blended the colours to your liking. You may well have to do this five or six times to achieve a good blend, but it gets quicker with practice. Experiment with different ratios of colours, and you can even blend the blends, making the range of colours and tones limitless!

> TIP: When brushing and mixing, be sure to brush one colour over another, to aid the mix. For example, if you lay two colours on the first brush side by side to blend, and keep brushing with the brushes in line with each other, they won't mix well. Misalign your second brush so that it brushes one colour over another, or place the colours on top of each other.

Blending is not a quick exercise and should be managed very slowly and deliberately. If

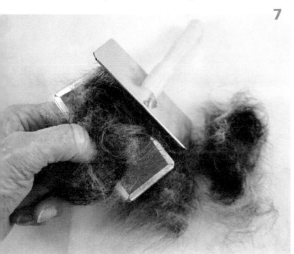

7

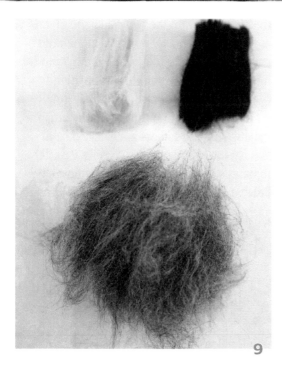

9

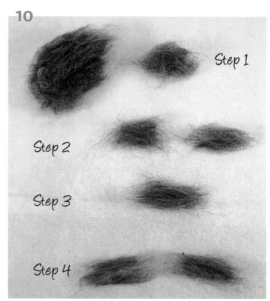

Step 1
Step 2
Step 3
Step 4

you are very rough with the carding, you will break the delicate fibres making them shorter. **9**

You should now have an evenly blended amount of Merino in a shade of your making. Before you can start attaching this to your sculpture, there is one final process. **10**

- Step 1: Pull a small amount from the blended Merino between your thumb and forefinger.
- Step 2: With both thumb and forefingers, pull that amount apart.
- Step 3. Place back together, one on top of the other.
- Step 4. Pull apart again.

Repeat this process a couple of times and you will notice that the Merino fibres will align and look more 'fur-like'. Each of these amounts in Step 4 are just perfect for general fur attachment. I sometimes arrange a row of these, ready to attach and to save a little time.

You can even create rough and smooth blends, rough being "just" blended so you can easily see which colours have been used and a "smooth" blend where you can't see which

colours have been used. For example, the Scotch Collie coat shown below was created with only using three colours of Merino wool, a black, sand and rich tan! (white was only used for the white colouring, not for blending) From those three colours, an extra four colours were created ranging from a smooth blend, shown in the tail and trousers (the fluffy part at the top of the back legs) to rough blends, as can be seen on the top of the tail and around the head, for different effects to make a lovely sable colouring.

Happy blending.

11

FUR ATTACHMENT

FUR ATTACHMENT

This short chapter shows how long fur is attached to a felted sculpture. Knowing how to do this will transform your work and give it a taxidermic appearance. You can simply attach solid colours, or you can spend some time and blend a range of colours. In fact, Merino wool is perfect for this as it comes is a huge range of colours, all of which can be blended together in various ratios to achieve a huge colour palette, as good as any painter! Almost any type of wool can be attached to create long fur, but by far the best for effect and versatility is Merino.

There are two basic methods: the across-the-middle and the end-attachment, sometimes referred to as shingling, due it being not unlike roof shingles.

ACROSS-THE-MIDDLE ATTACHMENT
1

The across-the-middle, as the name implies, is where the line of attachment is straight across the middle of the fibres. You take your length of Merino, which should be at least two and half times the finished length you require, lay it over where you want it attached, but with half the length placed in

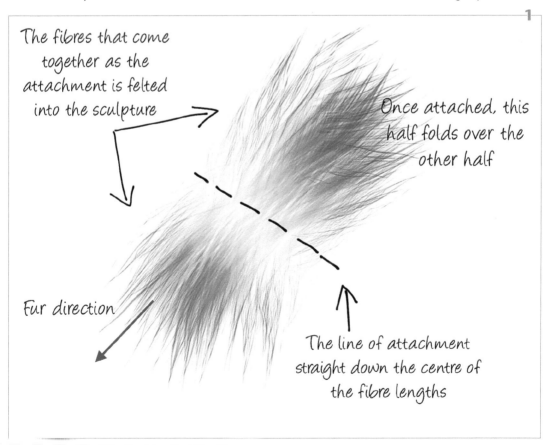

1

The fibres that come together as the attachment is felted into the sculpture

Once attached, this half folds over the other half

Fur direction

The line of attachment straight down the centre of the fibre lengths

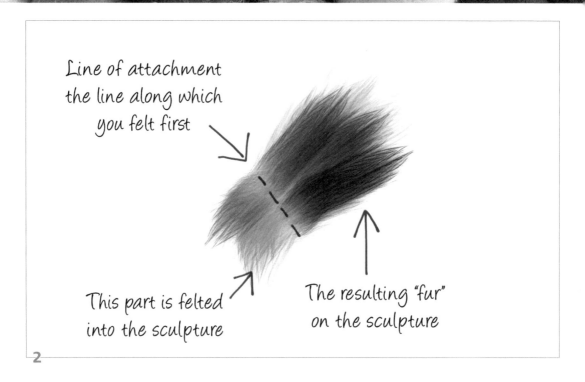

Line of attachment
the line along which
you felt first

This part is felted
into the sculpture

The resulting "fur"
on the sculpture

2

the direction of final fur. Once felted into place the other half will be placed over it. So if you wanted a final coat length of say 1cm (0.39in) then you have to allow for the part that will be felted into the sculpture which would be around 2 to 3mm (0.08 to 0.11in) and for trimming to shape and length another 3mm (0.11in) so roughly for a length of 1cm (0.39in) you would need a Merino length of 2.5cm (0.98in) However, carded Merino wool has limits of length, and would not be suitable for a very long coat. You would need some other wool for that.

Across-the-middle method is useful if you need to cover a large area quickly and have a good fairly deep surface of core wool on which to attach. Take care not to try and attach thick clumps of wool as this will prove difficult and will not attach easily. Instead use thin amounts that easily felt into the body.

You will notice as you felt along the line of attachment, both sides of the length of Merino will come together as the middle of the length is felted into the body. This is a good sign and shows that the attachment is

working. If you use your felting needle at a slight angle as you attach, (rather than felting directly down at 90° angle) you should find this works quickly. With the centre felted into the sculpture, lay the attachment as you desire. You can if you like lightly felt along the edge of the folded length if you need a flat attachment, or you can leave it as it is.

END ATTACHMENT (OR SHINGLE ATTACHMENT)
2, 3

This method is perfect for areas that are difficult to work on, or where you want more detail and finer control. You will need to cut lengths that are only 0.5cm (0.19in) longer than the finished length. For example, if you wanted a final coat length of 1cm (0.39in) you would need a wool length of 1.5cm (0.59in) Again, use thin amounts, and this time lay it only part-way over where you need to attach it, so that the longer length (the final fur) is laying in the final direction you want. With the excess, felt along the line of attachment, to stabilise the placement, then

106

3

felt into the sculpture any excess left over, leaving only the length you want.

Photo 3 shows both methods of fur attachment on the Snow Leopard, with the Merino shown in red and the line of attachment in blue.

GLOSSARY

Alcohol pens
A dye in pen form that can be used to colour a range of materials, including wool and acrylic beads, even clay.

Armature
A wire frame that offers support and guidance for size and proportions throughout the creation process.

Awl
A thin metal pointed tool with a handle, used to assist with delicate tiny-sized items.

Cabochon
A lens which is circular, crystal clear and has two sides, one convex the other flat, perfect for making eyes, when a printed eye is glued to the underside to show through the lens.

Carders
Two flat, metal-toothed brushes, used to card or 'brush' wool, either to make it fluffy or to blend colours together. They are always used in pairs.

Core wool (batts US)
Fleece that has been cleaned of any debris, washed to remove the lanolin, and carded (brushed) to make it fluffy and uniform. Core wool can also be processed into slivers, long lengths, that can be used in the same way as normal core.

Felting brush
A square long-bristled brush, used with the bristles facing up, on which flat felting can be achieved and normally used in conjunction with a multi-needle (sprung-type).

Glossy Accents/Diamond Glaze
Clear three-dimensional gloss mediums. Used to gloss the eye beads. As it is water based, it doesn't mix with the alcohol colours it is being used to seal.

Mod Podge
A large range of water-based decoupage mediums, an all-in-one glue, sealer and finish that can be used in a range of crafting applications, including needle felting.

Multi-needles
- Open multi-needle tool – A needle holder that can hold any number of needles, usually arranged in a circle.
- Sprung multi-needle tool – Another multi-needle holder, that can hold five or seven needles, encased in a sprung shield.
- Three-in-one needle tool - One of my favourite tools, with three needles placed in a row.

Pan pastels
Super soft pastels in a 'pan'; these can be applied with a paint brush to add colour detailing to your sculpture. Pigments are very strong and long-lasting.

Pins
Two types of pins are used in this book, ordinary round-headed sewing pins, useful for placing

the open nostrils on an animal's nose, and the longer thicker large-headed pins, also called hat pins. These are essential for the placement of ears, to ensure they are correct, level and in the right pose, before felting them onto the sculpture. They are also very helpful in placing the feet on the base on a felting sponge whilst you sew each foot in turn to the base.

Polymer clay
A type of clay that can be moulded into any shape, then baked to 'cure' (to make it hard). The most popular brand of polymer clay is FIMO.

PVA glue
A white, clear-drying craft glue, adequate for most needle felting needs, used to glue eyes in place, nails into toes, noses onto muzzles and wool onto clay.

Pyrography pen or wood burning pen
A pen-like heating element, which has a variety of small shaped attachments that are heated to an iron temperature. Can be used to flatten and shape the surface of felted wool. The most useful attachment is the flat pointed one.

Reverse felt
Using a reverse needle, one which has the barbs in the opposite direction to normal felting needles, to either blend layers of

different coloured wools, or to fluff the surface of felted wool.

Rubber-tipped clay tools
A range of tools with soft rubber tips, which have a more gentle touch with the clay. They are particularly useful in applying Silk Clay eyelids.

Sculpting tools
A range of metal or rubber tipped tools, used to shape and texture clay.

Silk clay
A self hardening clay that dries at room temperature into a soft rubber-like texture.

Spacer beads
This is my own term. Any bead that can be used to form a perfect cavity for the coloured acrylic eye beads.

Spectrum Noir pens
A make of alcohol marker pen.

Tops (roving US)
Core wool (batts US) that has gone through a further industrial process. The fleece, having been washed and carded, is then combed and stretched out to straighten the fibres into what looks like 'combed hair' and is processed into long single lengths.

SUPPLIERS

World of Wool
www.worldofwool.co.uk

Adelaide Walker
www.adelaidewalker.co.uk

Felt Alive
www.feltalive.com

Felt Box (The)
www.thefeltbox.co.uk

Heidifeathers
www.heidifeathers.com

Makerss (The)
www.themakerss.co.uk

Mum's Makery
www.mumsmakery.co.uk

Sarafina Fibre Art
www.sarafinafiberart.com

Wizpick
www.wizpick.com

For anyone who would like to link up with other like-minded needle felters of dogs, I run a very active Facebook group, *Needle Felted DOGS*, on which you can show your work, ask questions about the subject, and share experiences. Existing members are friendly and helpful folk from around the world: from raw beginner to the most advanced felters, all are welcome.

Find me here –
www.chicktincreations.com
https://www.instagram.com/chicktincreations/
https://www.facebook.com/ChicktinCreations

When, in late 2018, World of Wool approached me to design some needle felting kits, I couldn't have been happier. Since then, I have written a kit every month, covering a wide range of animals.

All of the materials required are included in the kits, together with a detailed, step-by-step, photographic instructional booklet, and each teaches something new. The kits are extremely popular, and sell all around the world.

Learn to create hyper-realistic needle felted dogs, with step-by-step instructions and photos from start to finish. Written by a master of needle felting, the book details a range of methods for coat textures, shapes, finishes and realistic accessories.

Covering four different breeds of dog (Dachshund, Chihuahua, Yorkshire Terrier and Poodle), with step-by-step instructions and photos, Cindy takes you through the processes of creating different body shapes, proportions, armatures, coats, and blending, as well as realistic eyes, noses, mouths, ears, and nails.

Take your needle felting to the next level!

Paperback · ISBN: 978-1-787113-83-1

A
MASTERCLASS
in
NEEDLE FELTING WILDLIFE
METHODS AND TECHNIQUES TO TAKE YOUR NEEDLE FELTING TO THE NEXT LEVEL

Hubble & Hattie

Cindy-Lou Thompson

Learn how to create four hyper-realistic wild animals, with step-by-step instructions and photos from start to finish, written by a world class needle felting artist. The book shows how to make a range of armatures, coats, textures, shapes, and finishing touches, and gives step-by-step instructions for making Hare, Fox, Badger and an Otter models.
Take your needle-felting to a whole new level!

Paperback · ISBN: 978-1-787117-47-1

Available in the UK from www.veloce.co.uk or order worldwide from all major retailers